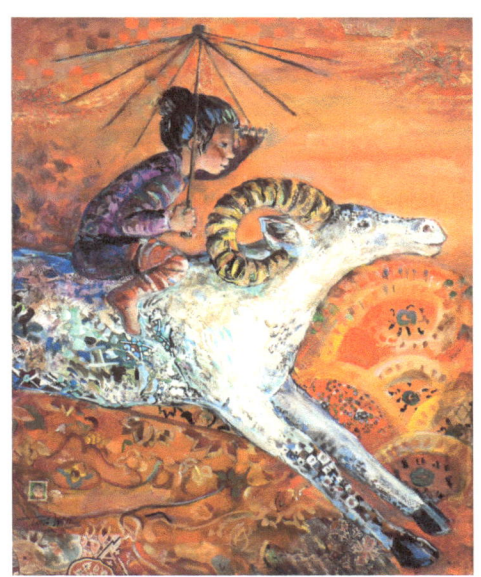

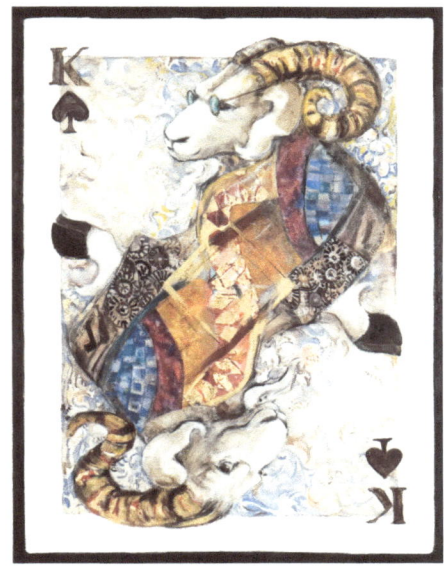

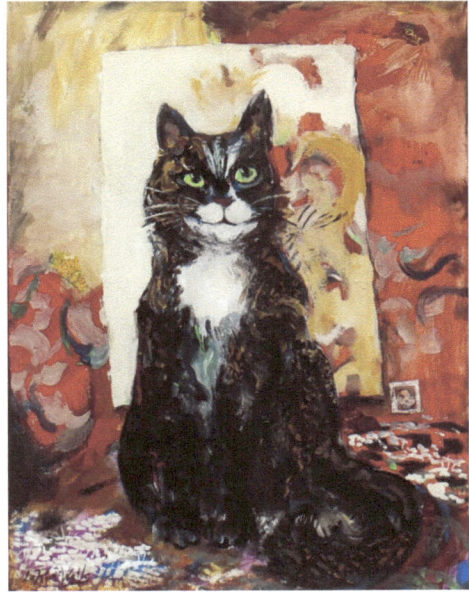

From an Inner Landscape

Mary LaRue Wells

From an Inner Landscape

©2010 by Mary LaRue Wells

ISBN 1451556276
EAN-13 9781451556278

Technical design and cover by Heinz Kagerer

Printed in the United States of America

About the Artist

Mary LaRue Wells' paintings have been unique and intriguing from the very start, her childhood knack for imaginary storytelling playing itself out in her art. She recalls constructing figures and drawing cards for her parents, and says she always knew art and painting was what she wanted to do.

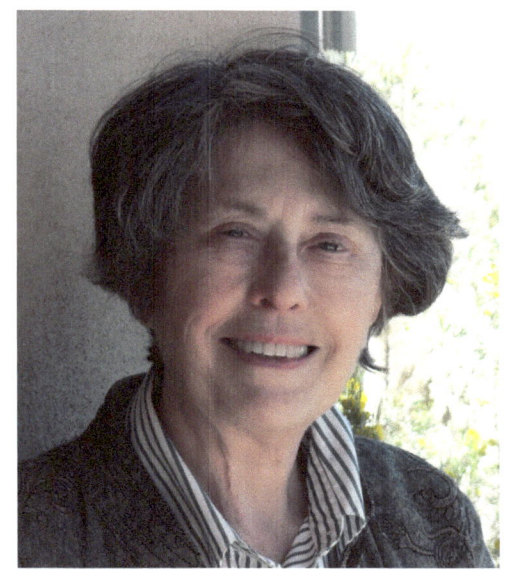

Mary now works in oils and acrylics, sometimes incorporating elements of collage with postage stamps and other paper items. Human and animal figures interact and converse as though on a stage, with lines the artist says may be quite quirky at times and surprise even herself. Some come from her "inner landscapes" while others may have roots in real life situations where unwitting subjects play out her dramas. Their worlds may be very complex at times, and gently surrealistic, woven together by patterns and symbols such as dice or eyeglasses that invite closer observation and interpretation.

Wells graduated from the University of Washington with a degree in Fine Arts and has participated in numerous juried competitions and exhibitions across the country. Her work has been included in Atelier A/E in New York City; Gallery K in Washington D.C.; Greater Reston Art Center in Reston, VA; Moonshell Gallery in Hilton Head, SC; Fountain City Art Center in Knoxville, TN, and on the Internet with Paradise Wild.

Wells now divides her time between Knoxville, TN and Scottsdale, AZ where she participated in the Hidden in the Hills studio tours.

BABIES

I hope you will enjoy this visual walk through three areas of my work. In the babies' series human figures may be quite young, but with my brush they become ageless, magical and wise.

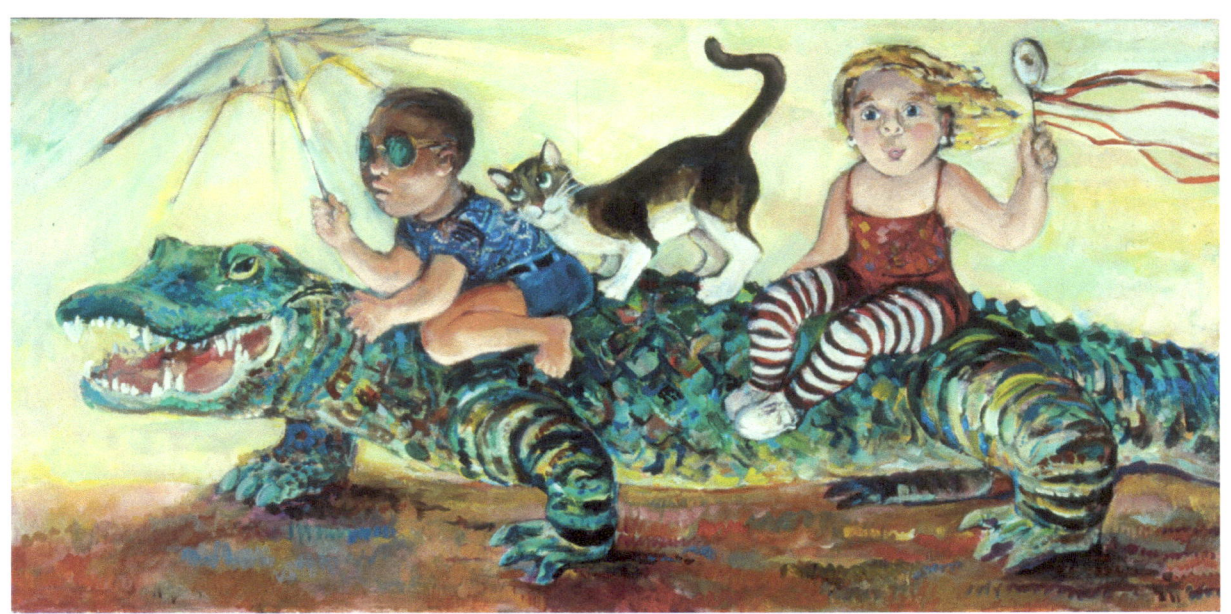

Big Al
24"x48"

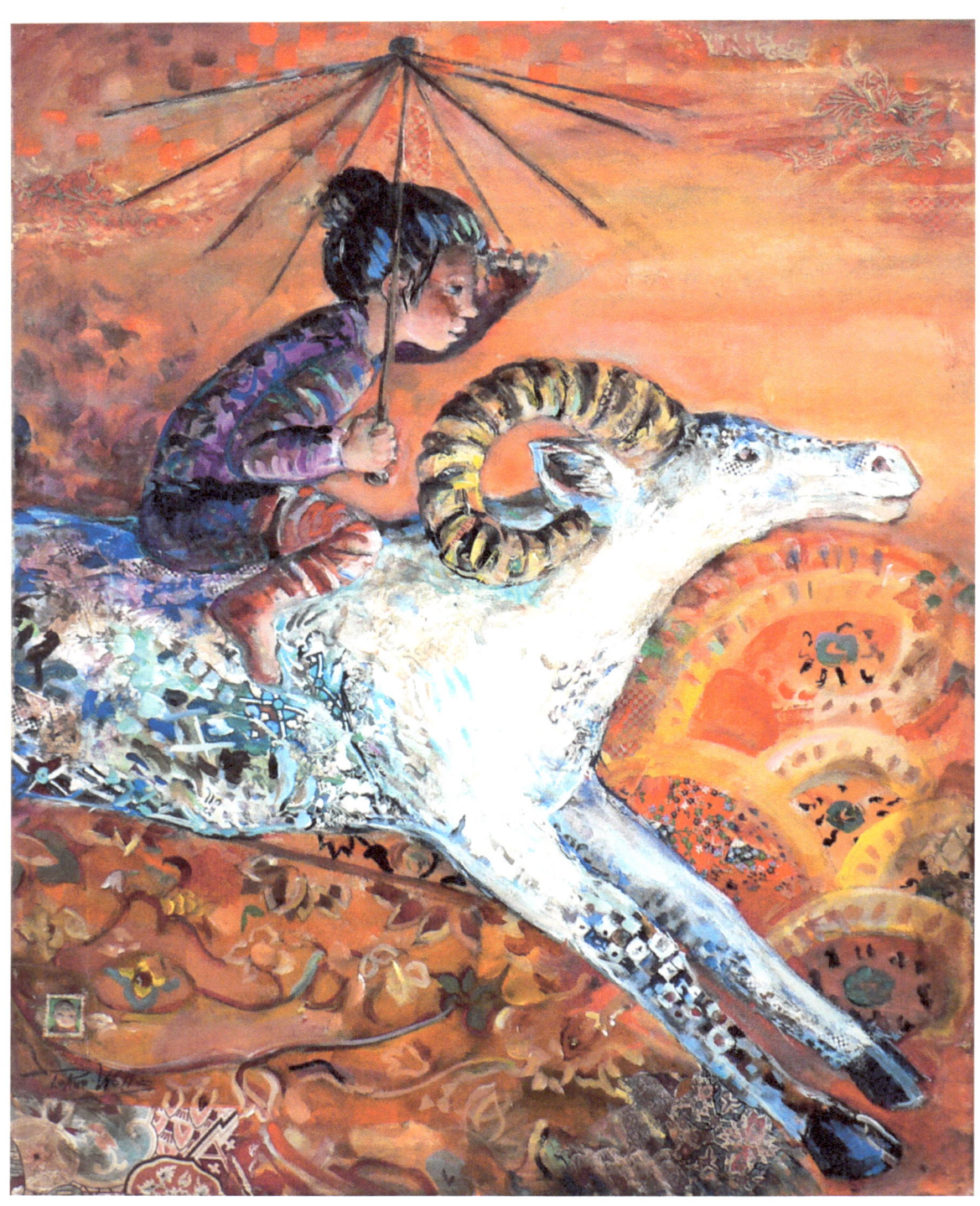

The Quest
30"x24"

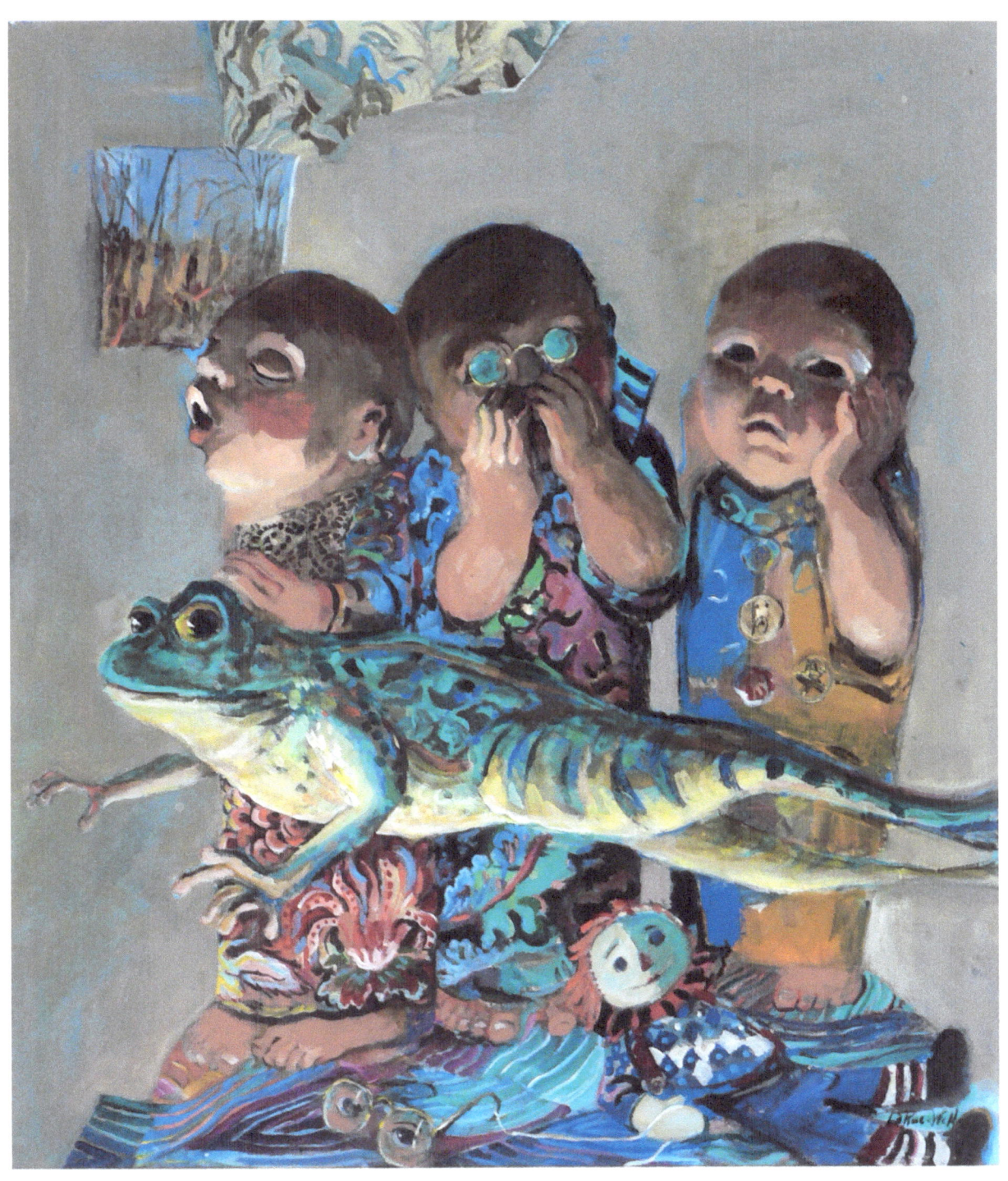

Jeté
24"x22"

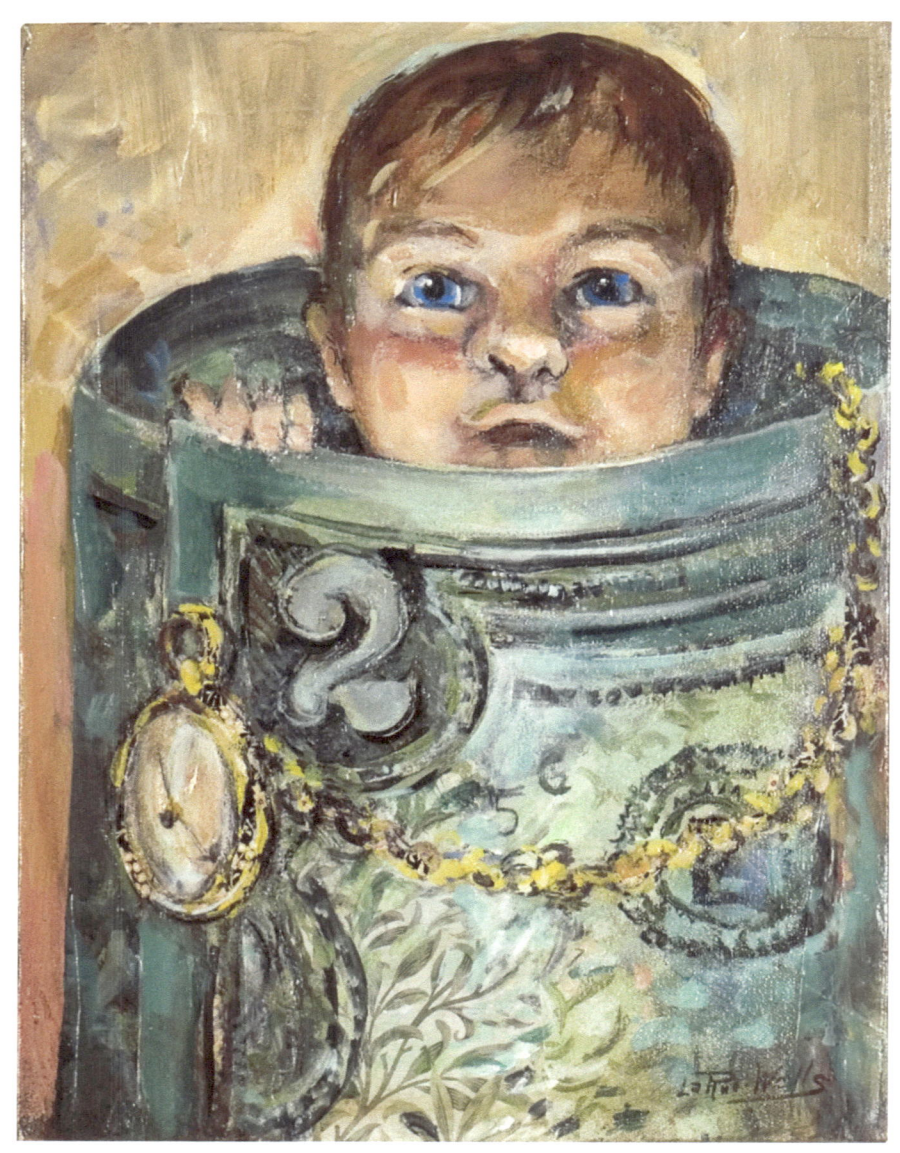

Two in Two
16"x12"

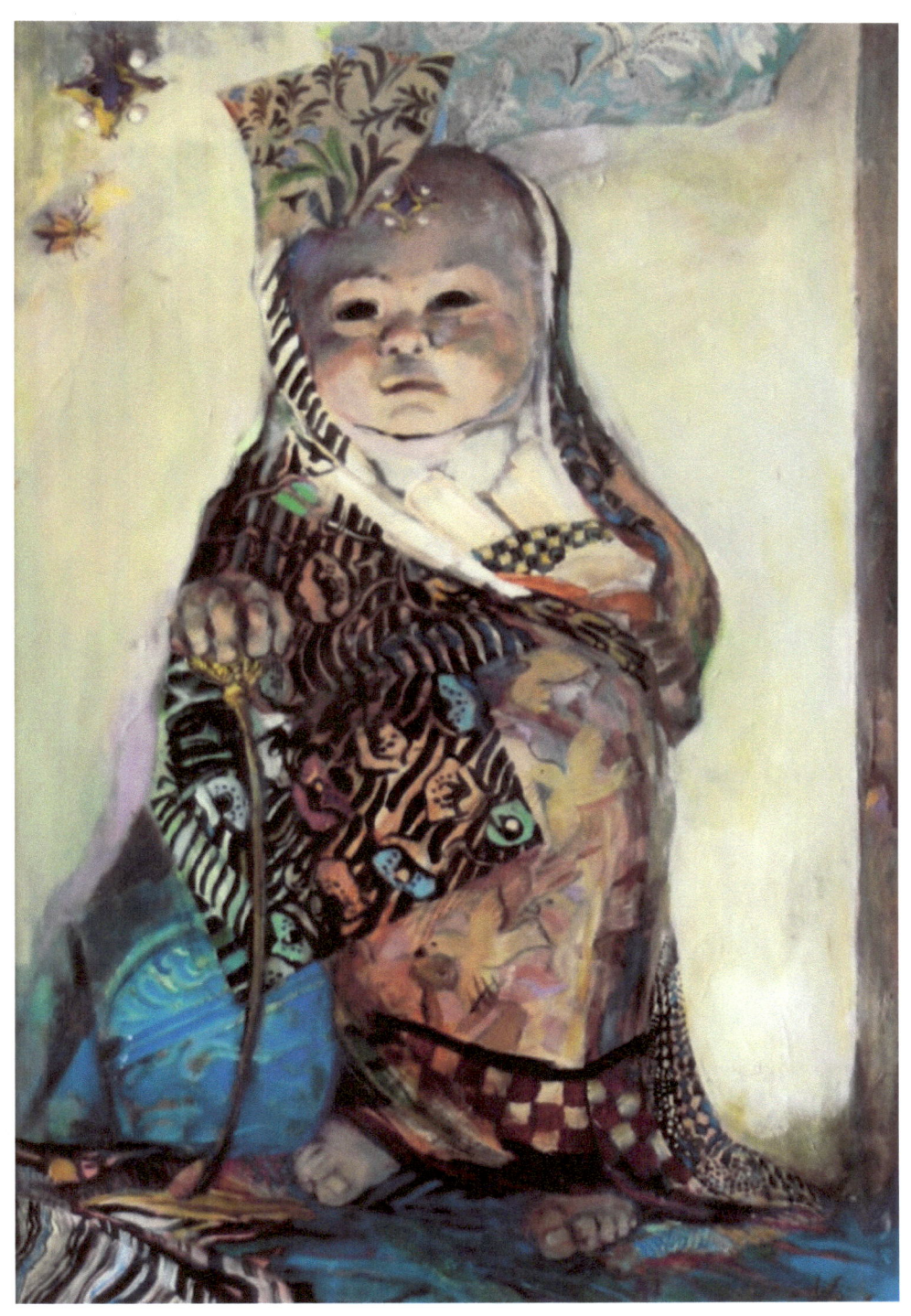

The Matriarch
22"x15"

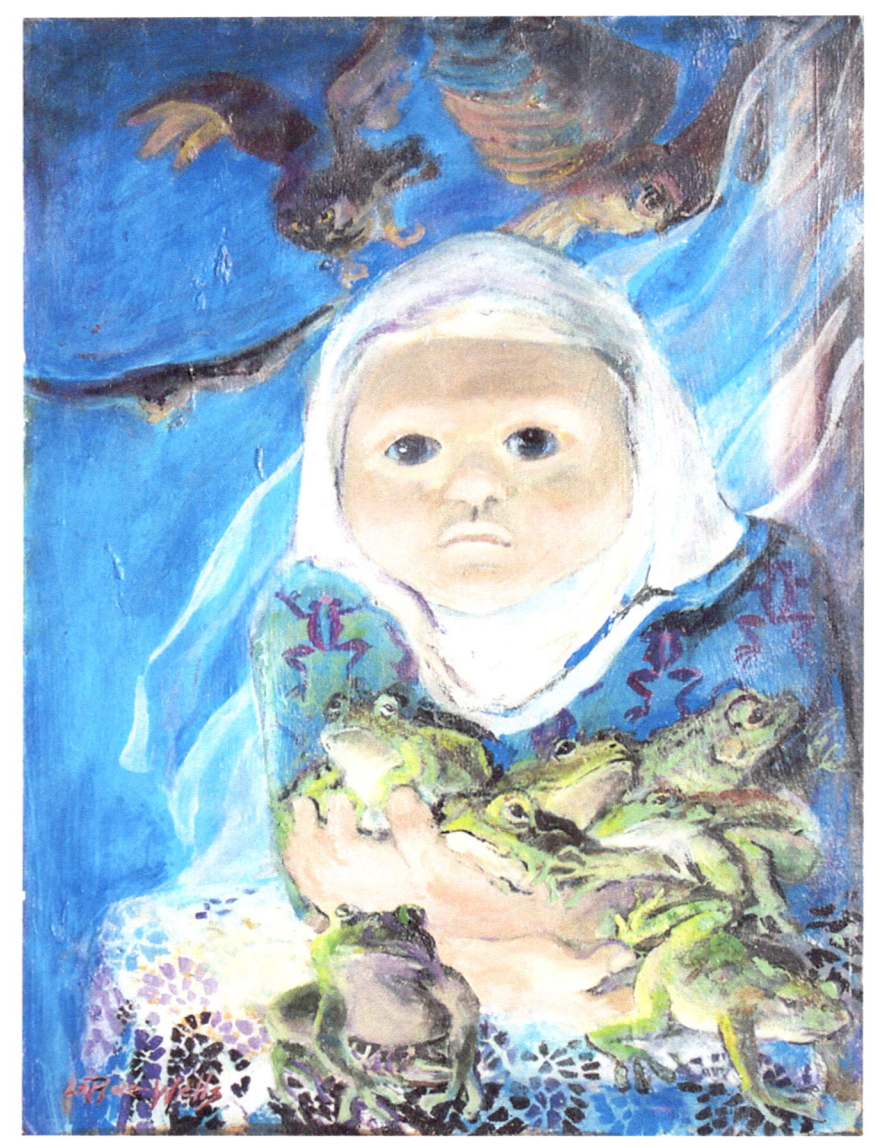

Protector
14"x11"

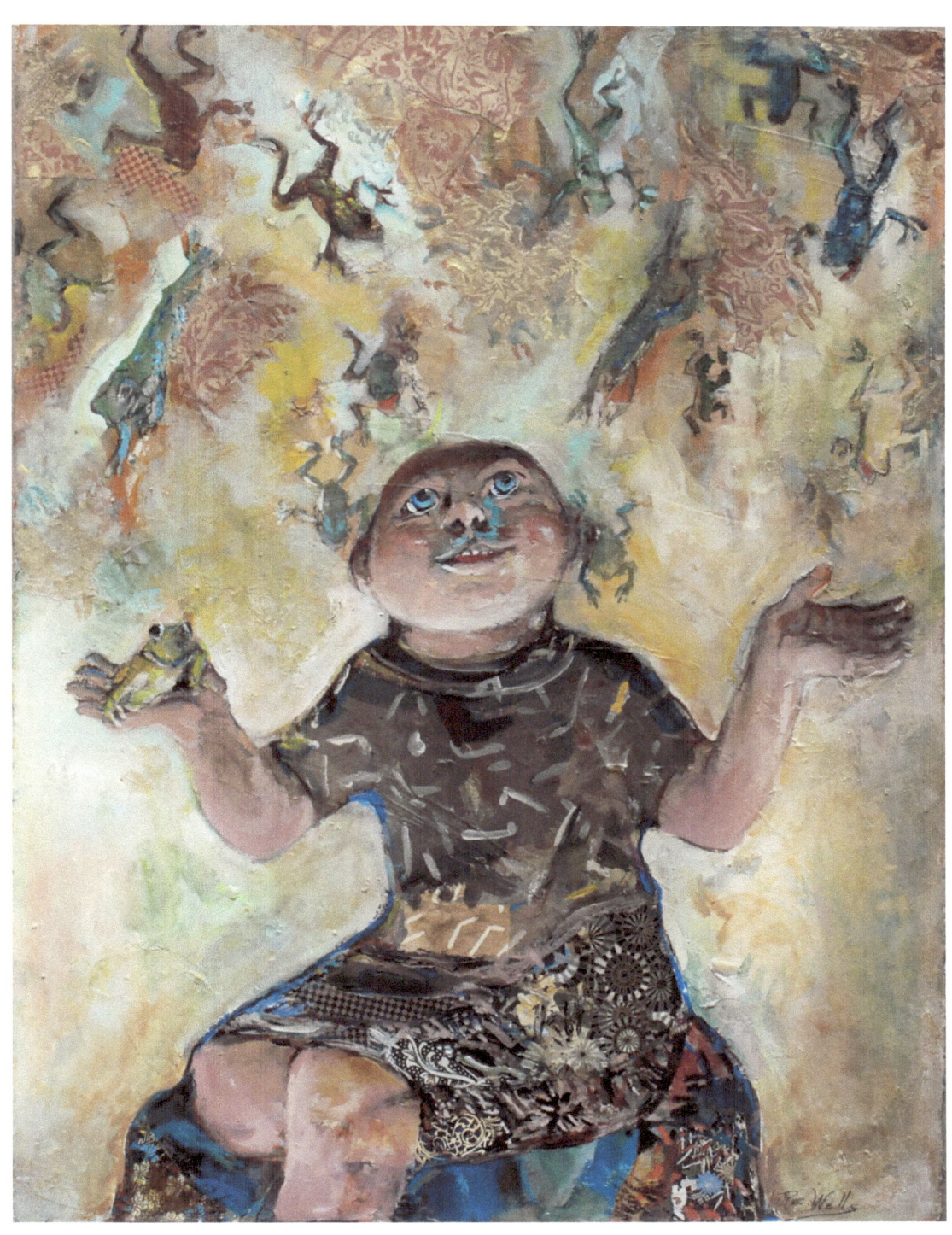

Raining Frogs
30"x24"

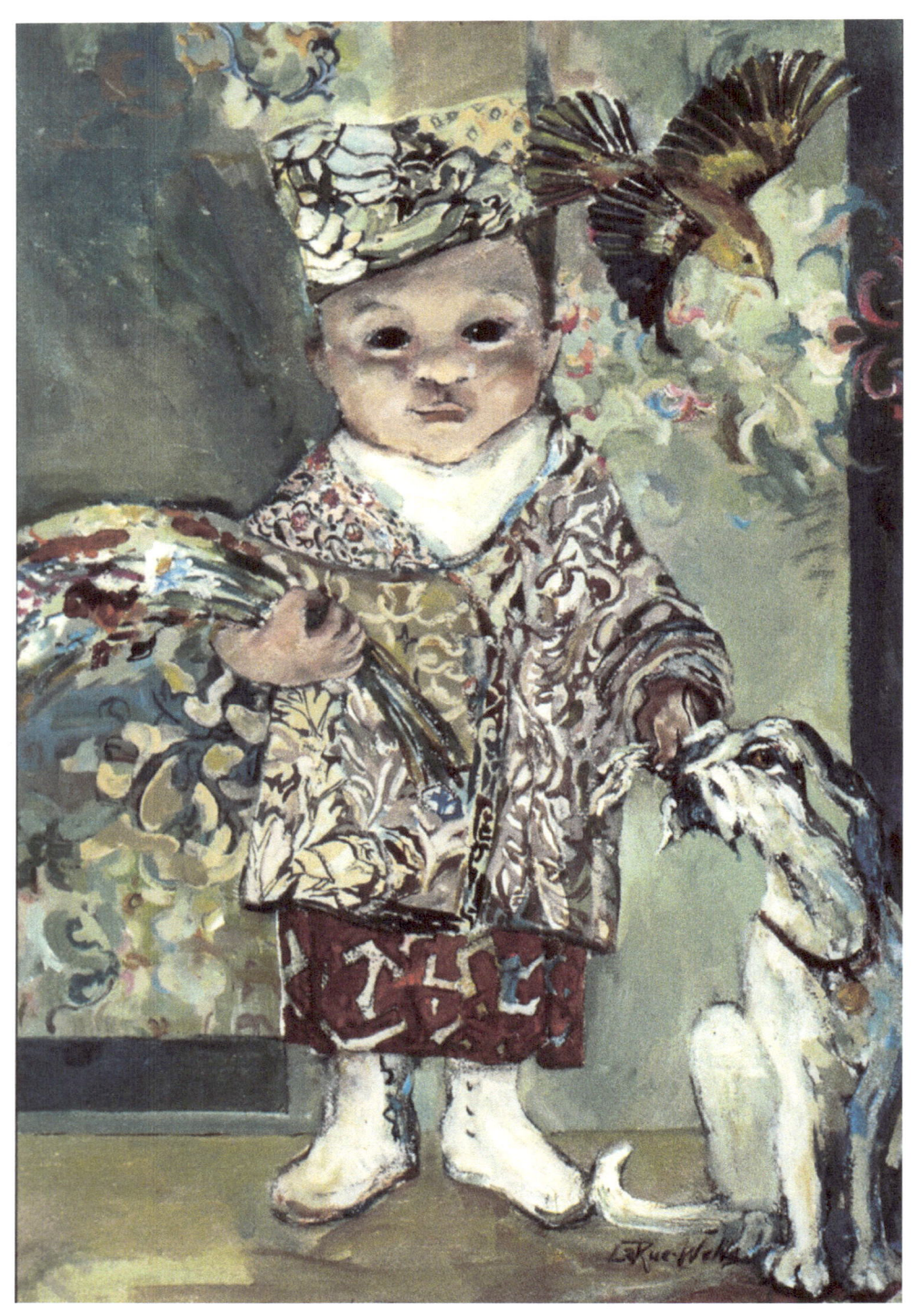

The Child Who Never Left Home
22"x15"

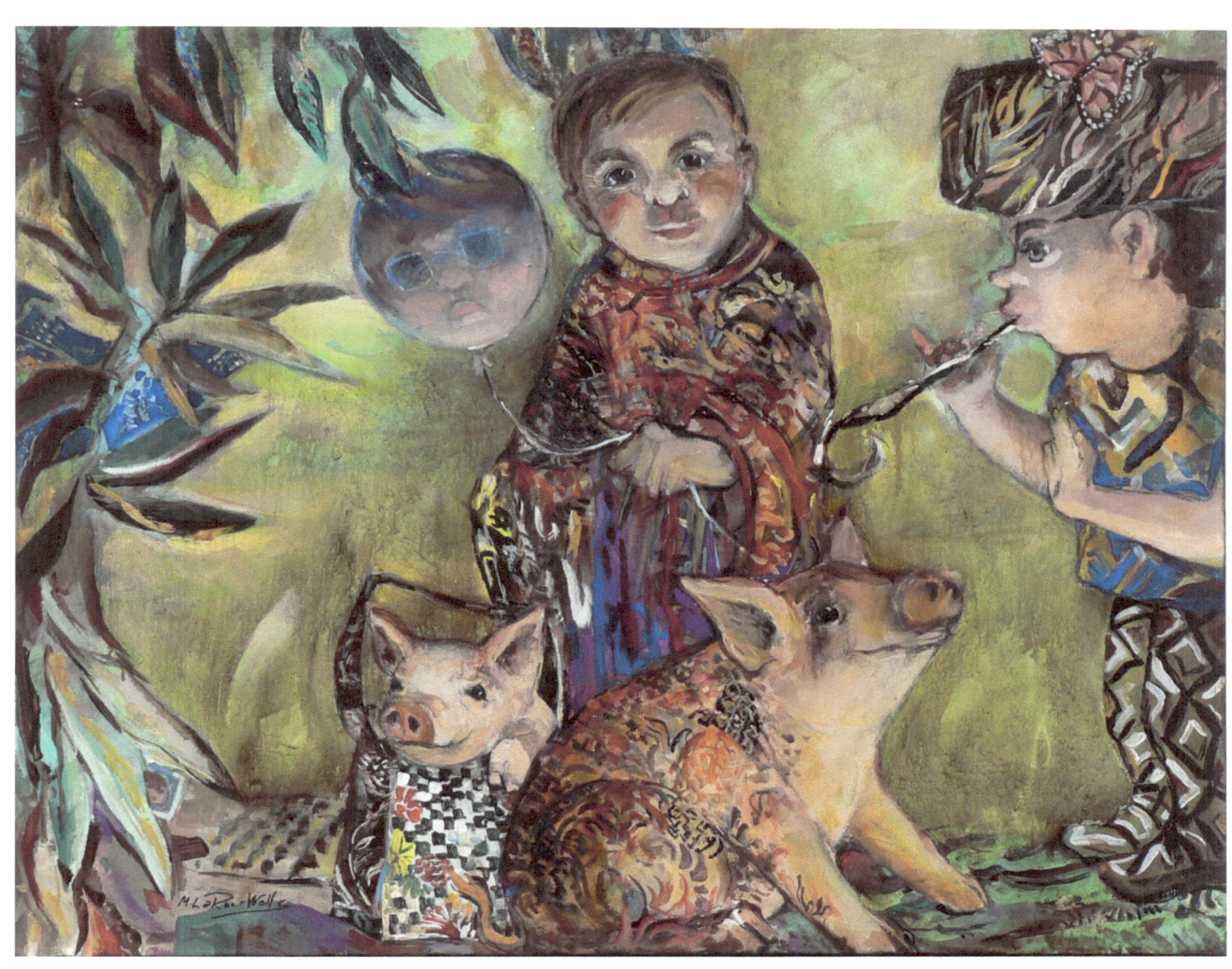

The Carnival
30"x24"

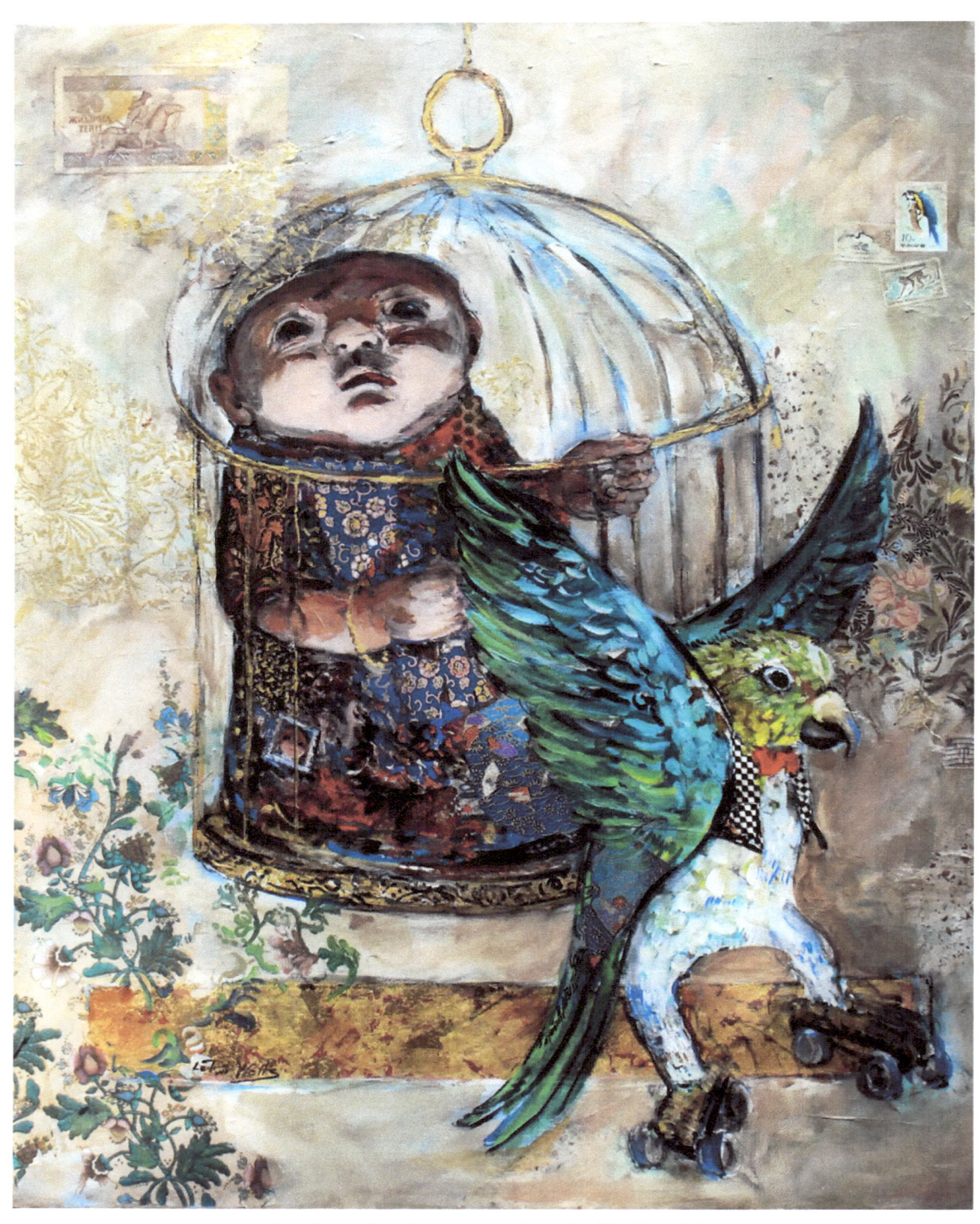

Seeing the Opportunity, Polly Took It
30"x24"

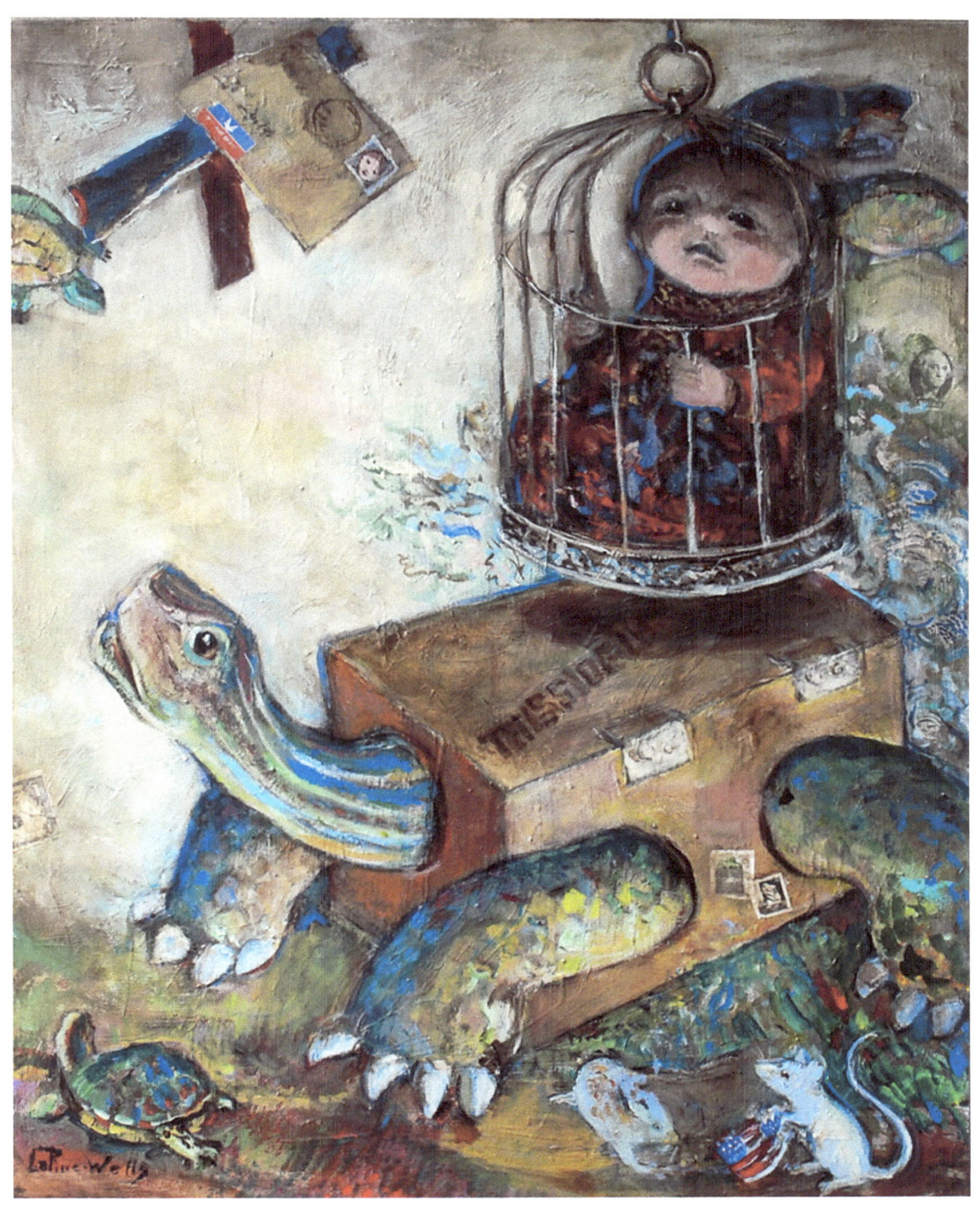

Turtle Express
30"x24"

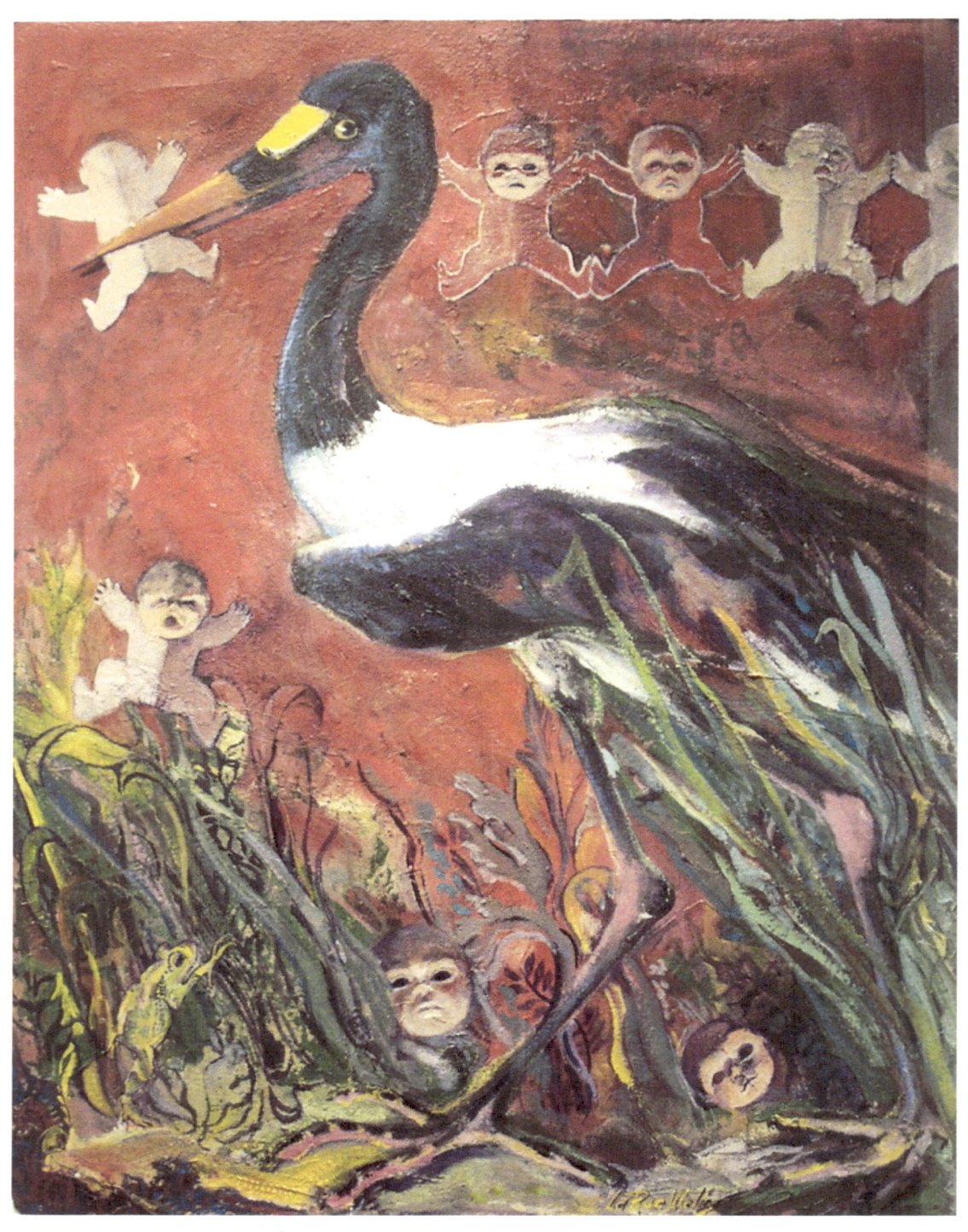

African Wood Stork Delivering Babies
25"x14"

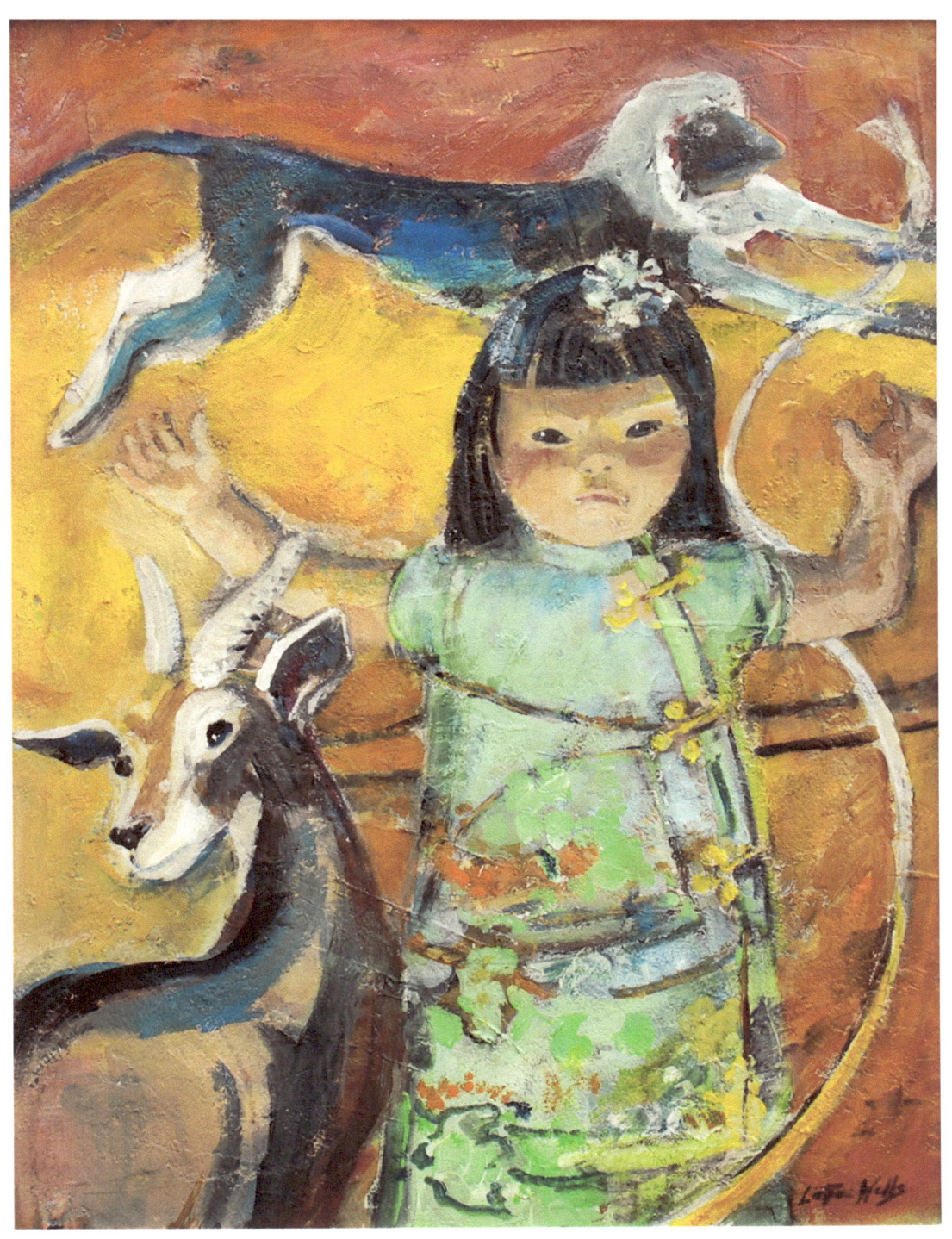

Center Ring
24"x18"

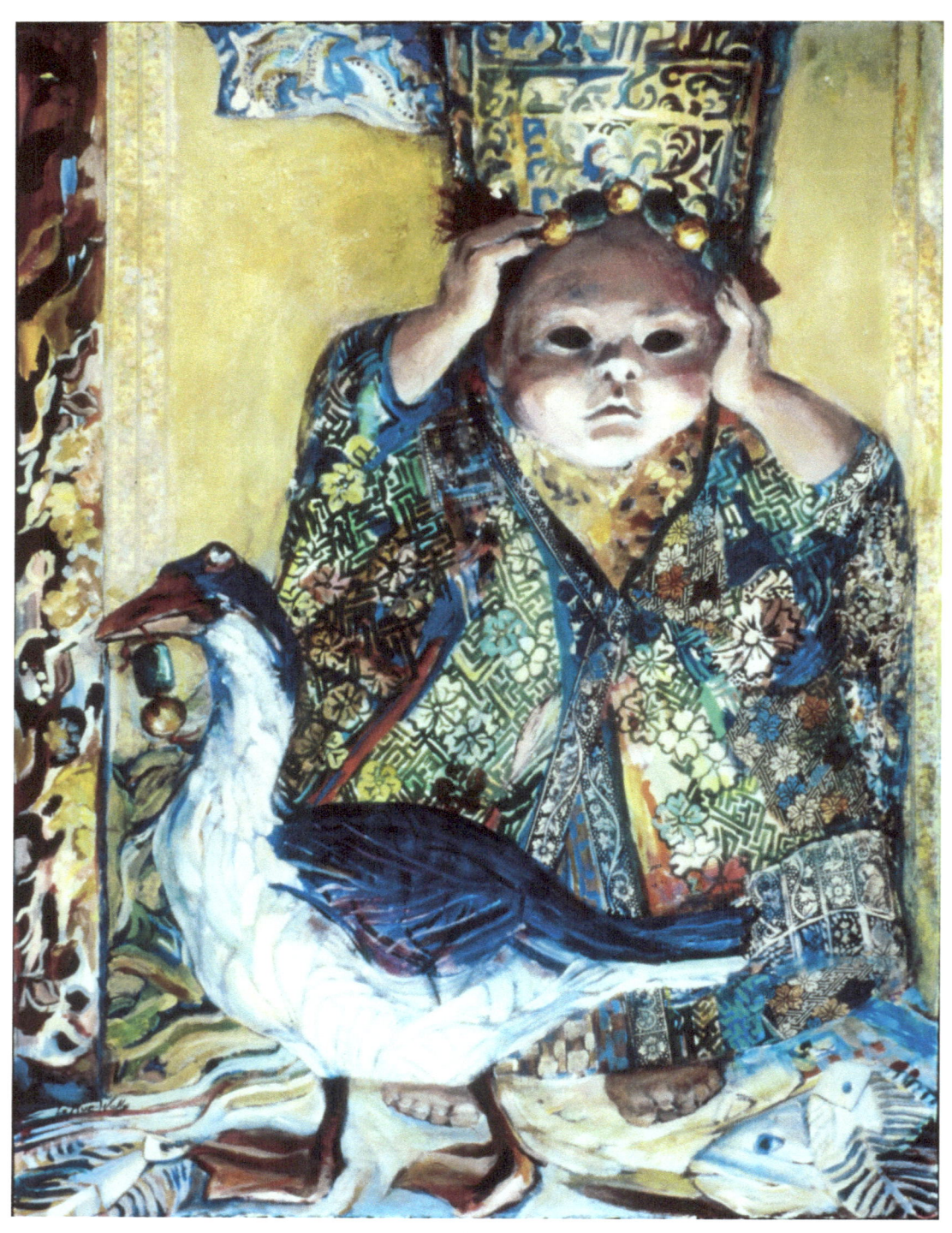

Royal Goose
22"x17"

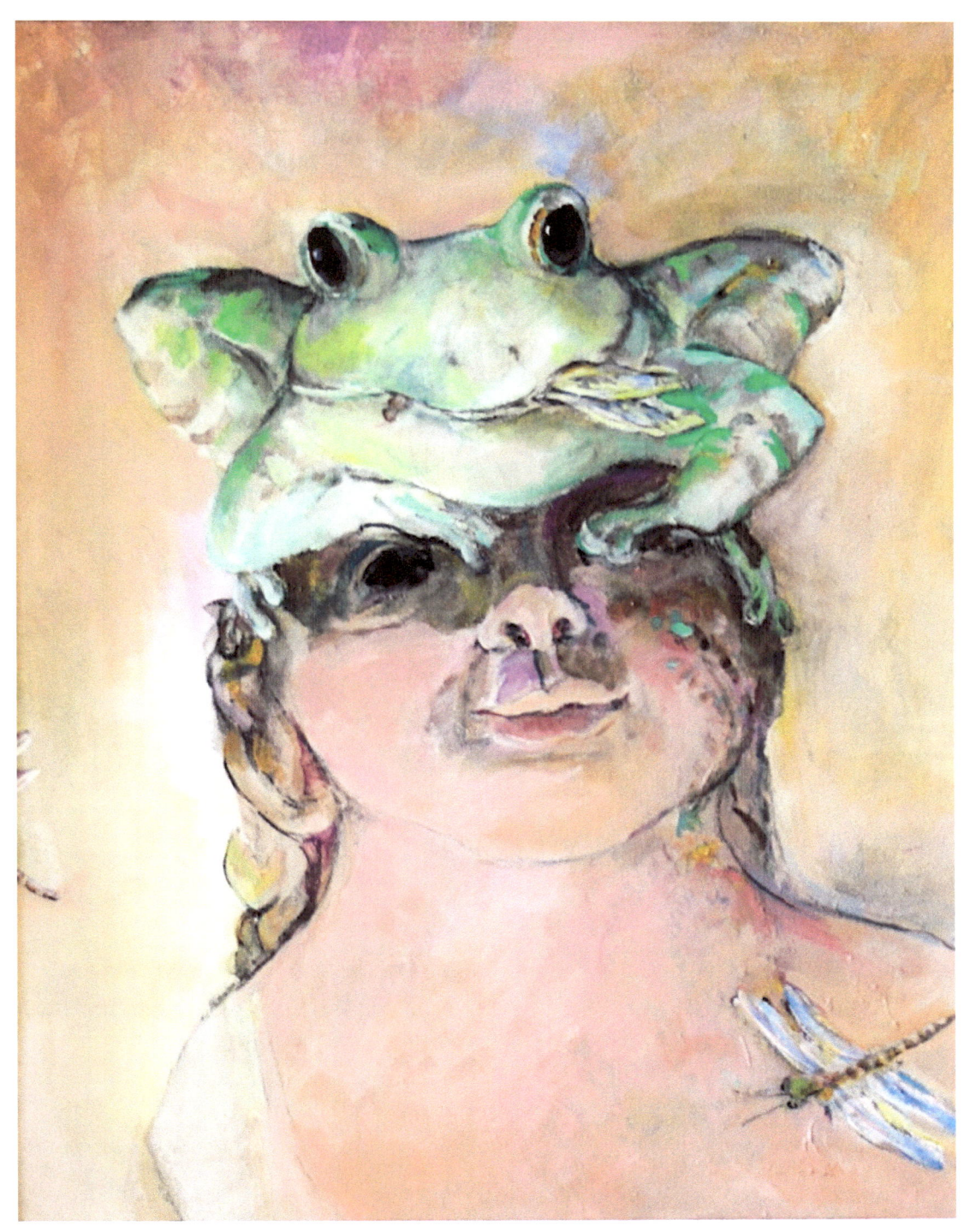

My Prince
20"x16"

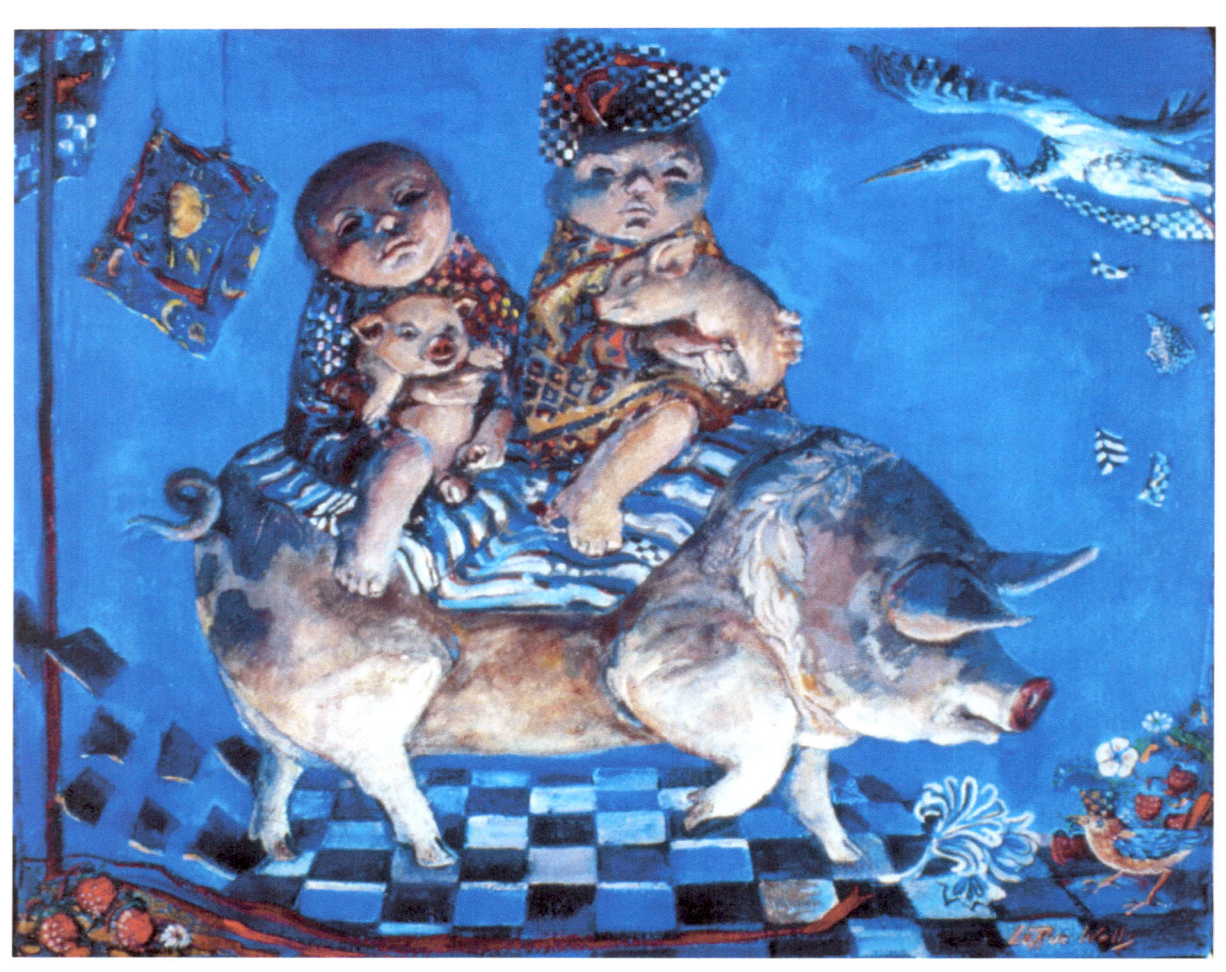

Night Journey
18"x22"

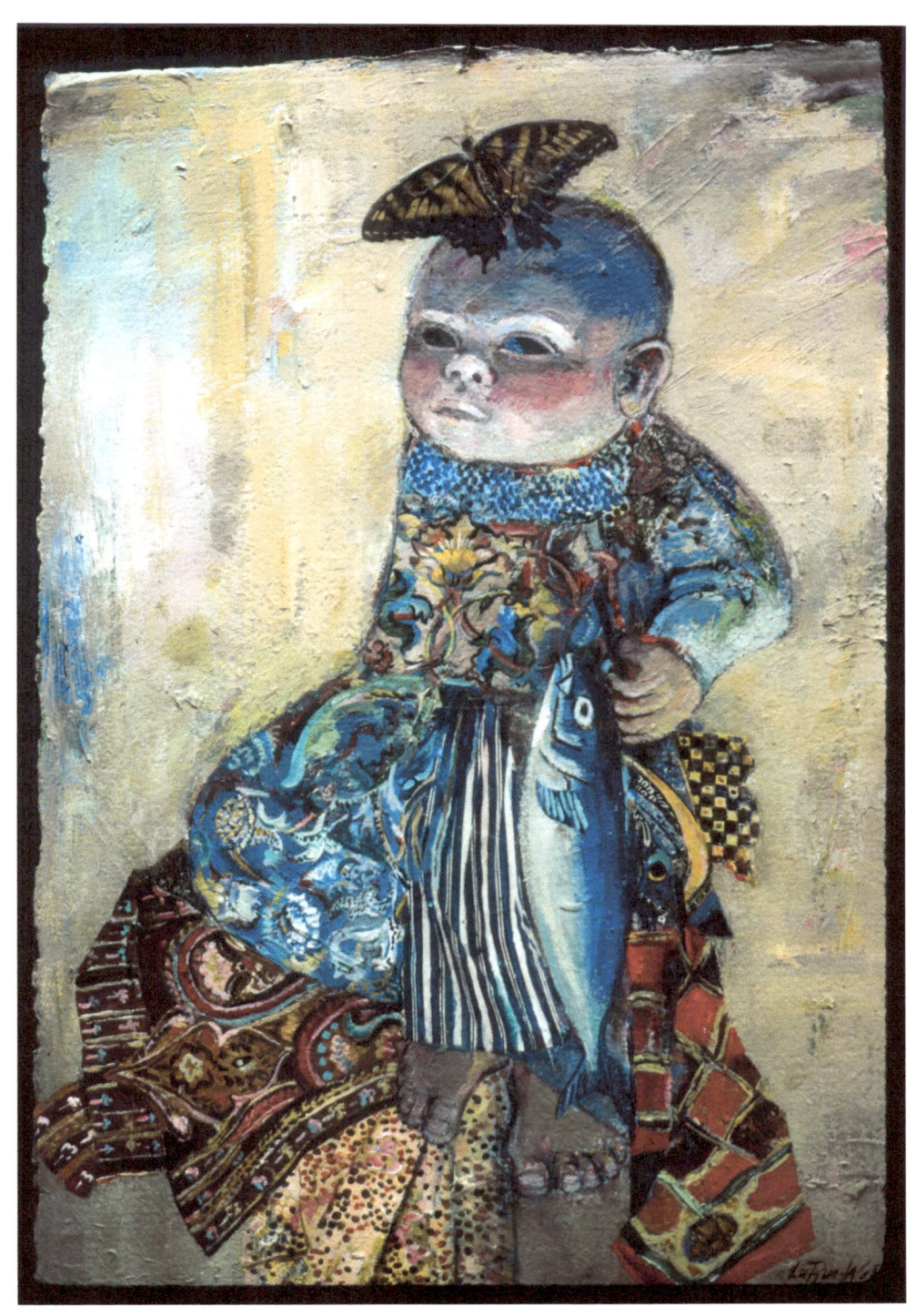

Monarc
22"x15"

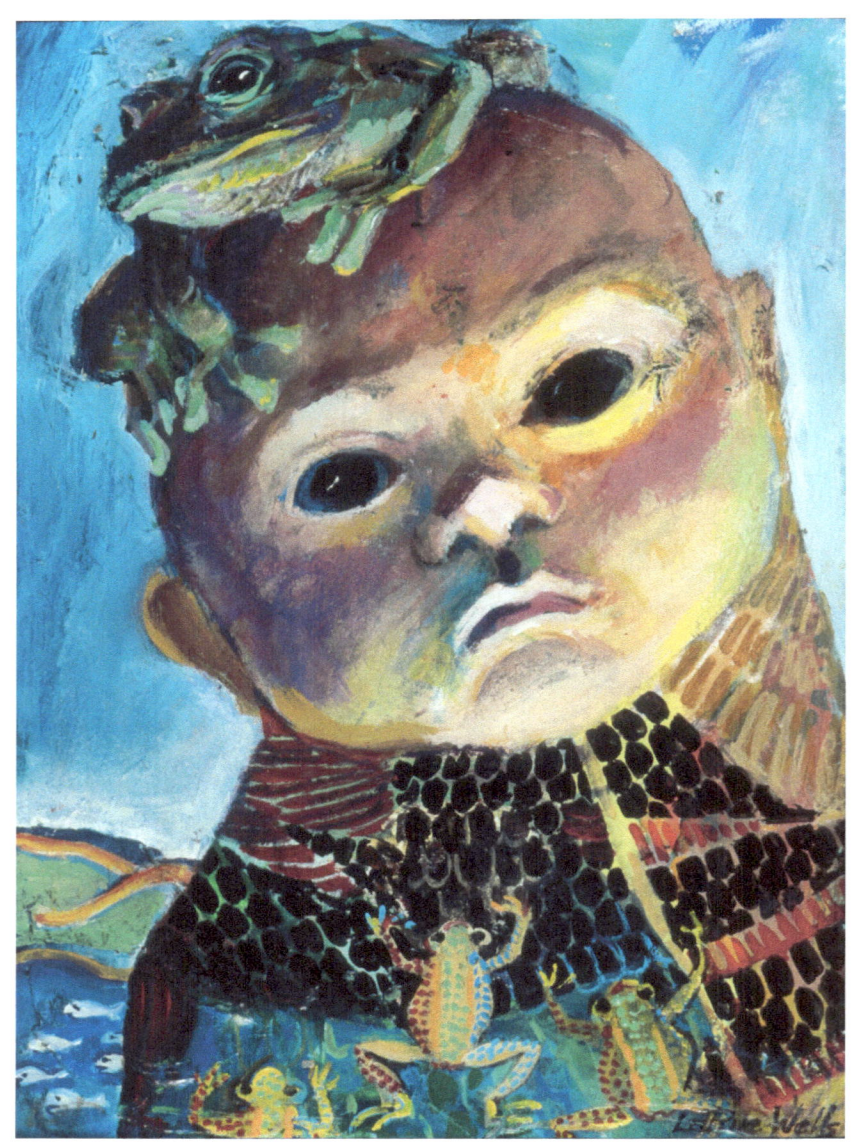

Top of the World
10"x7"

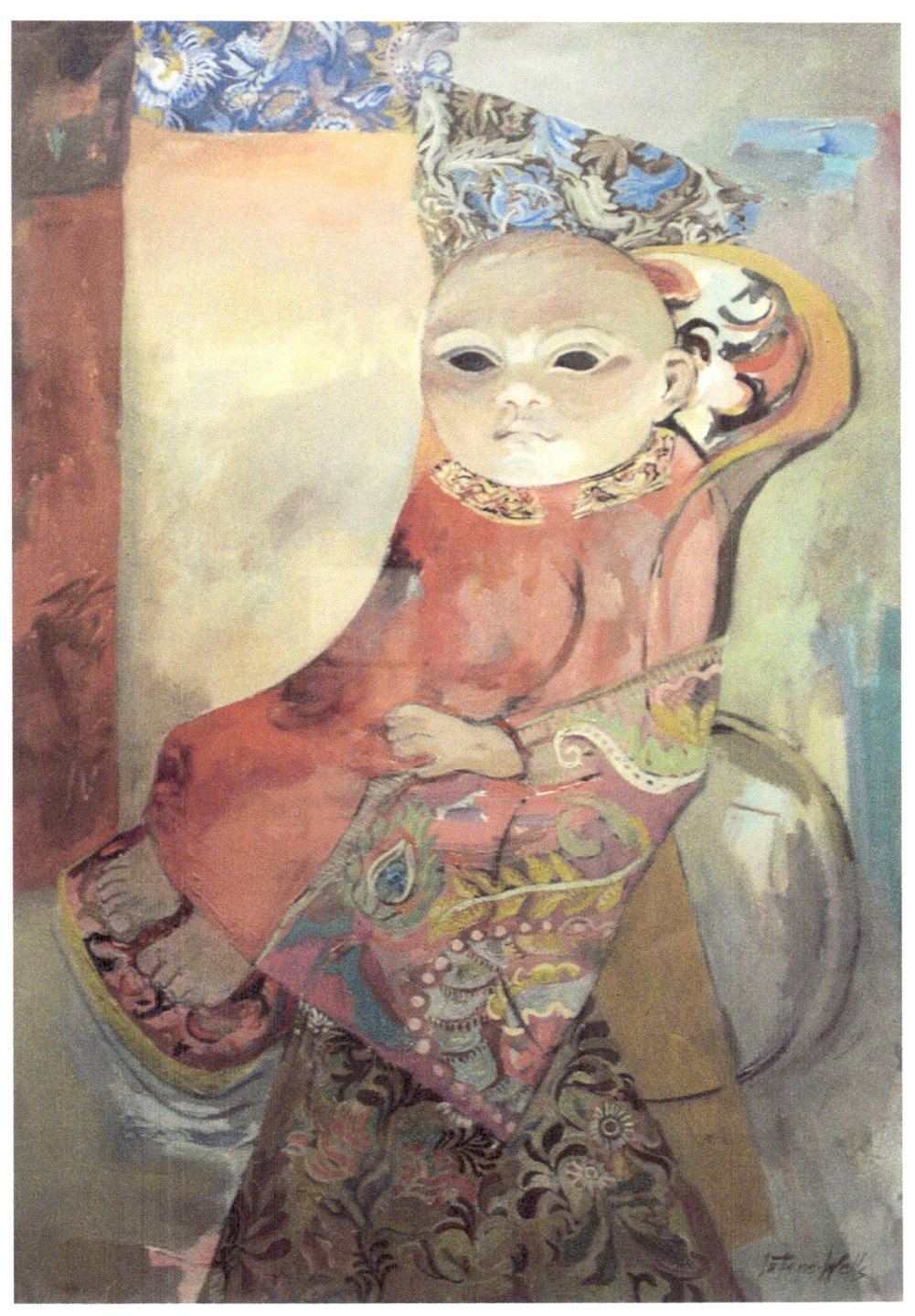

Fukothai I
22"x15"

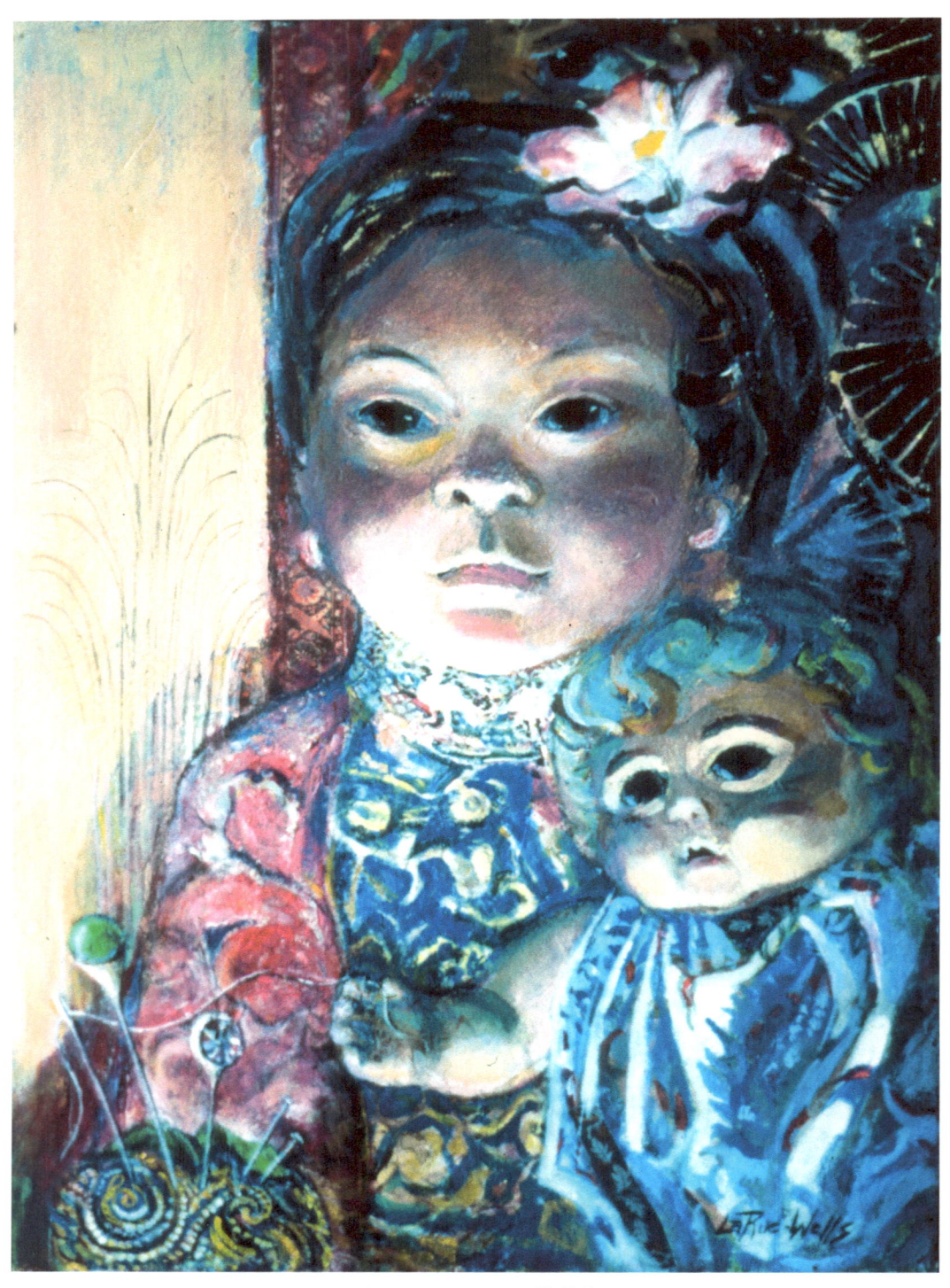

Once Upon a Child
14"x10"

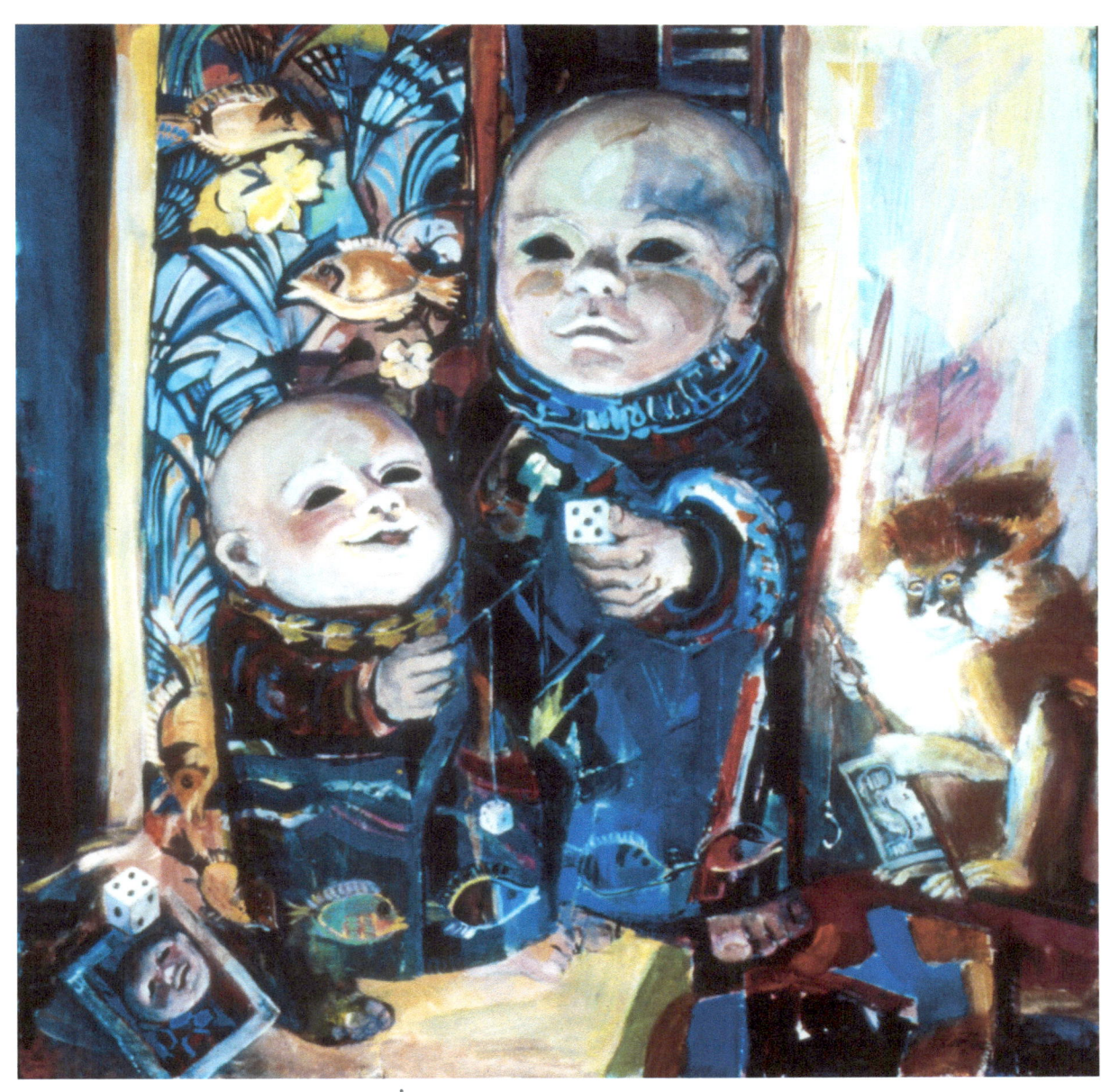

Monkey Business
22"x22"

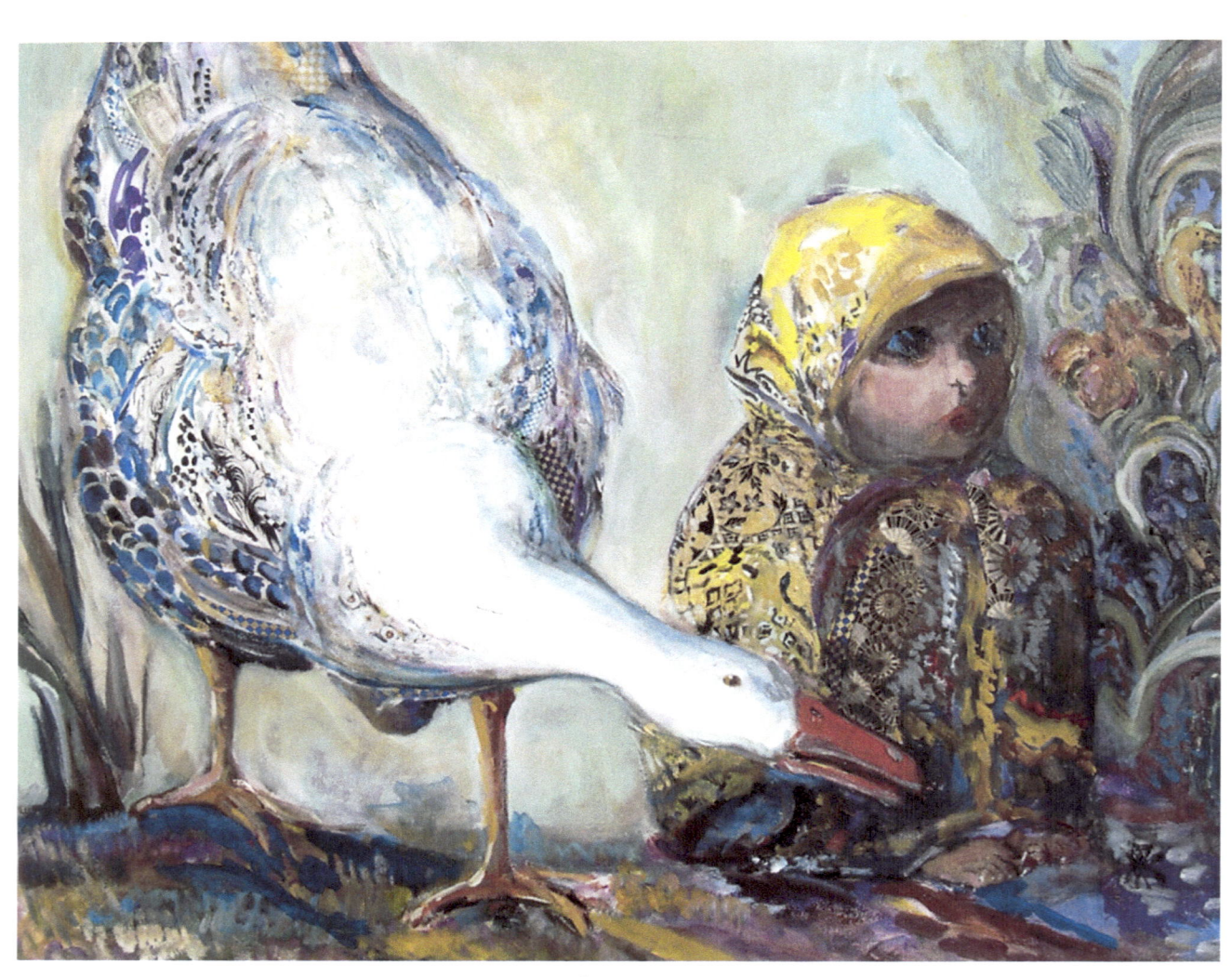

Mother Goose
22"x28"

CARDS

Recent work in my playing card series reveals animal
and human figures with greatly different personalities,
all depending on how you look at it.

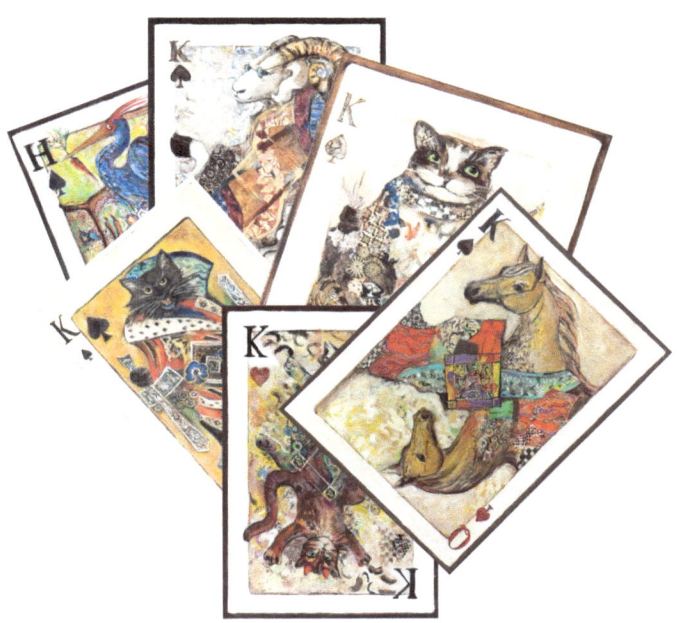

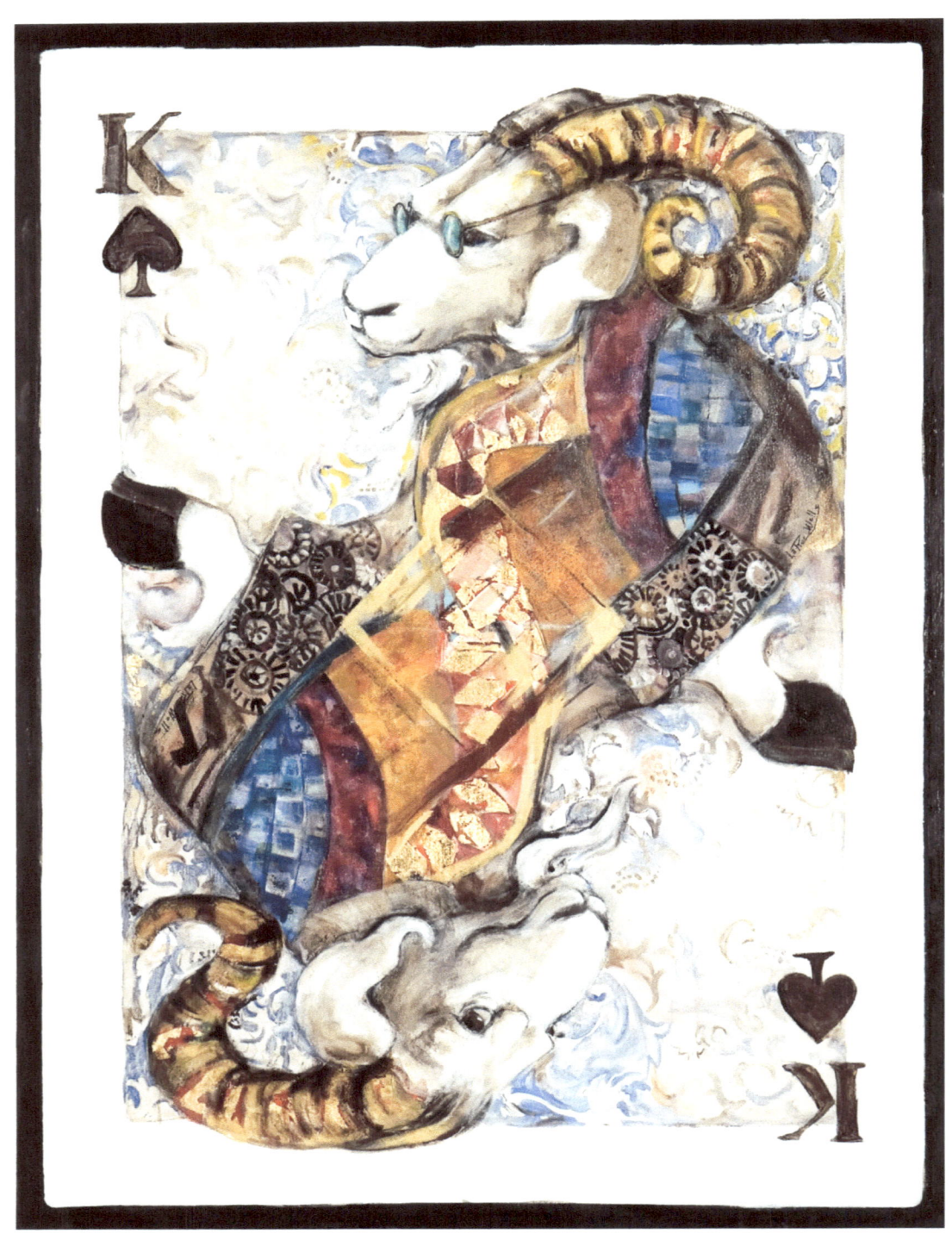

Ramses
48"x36"

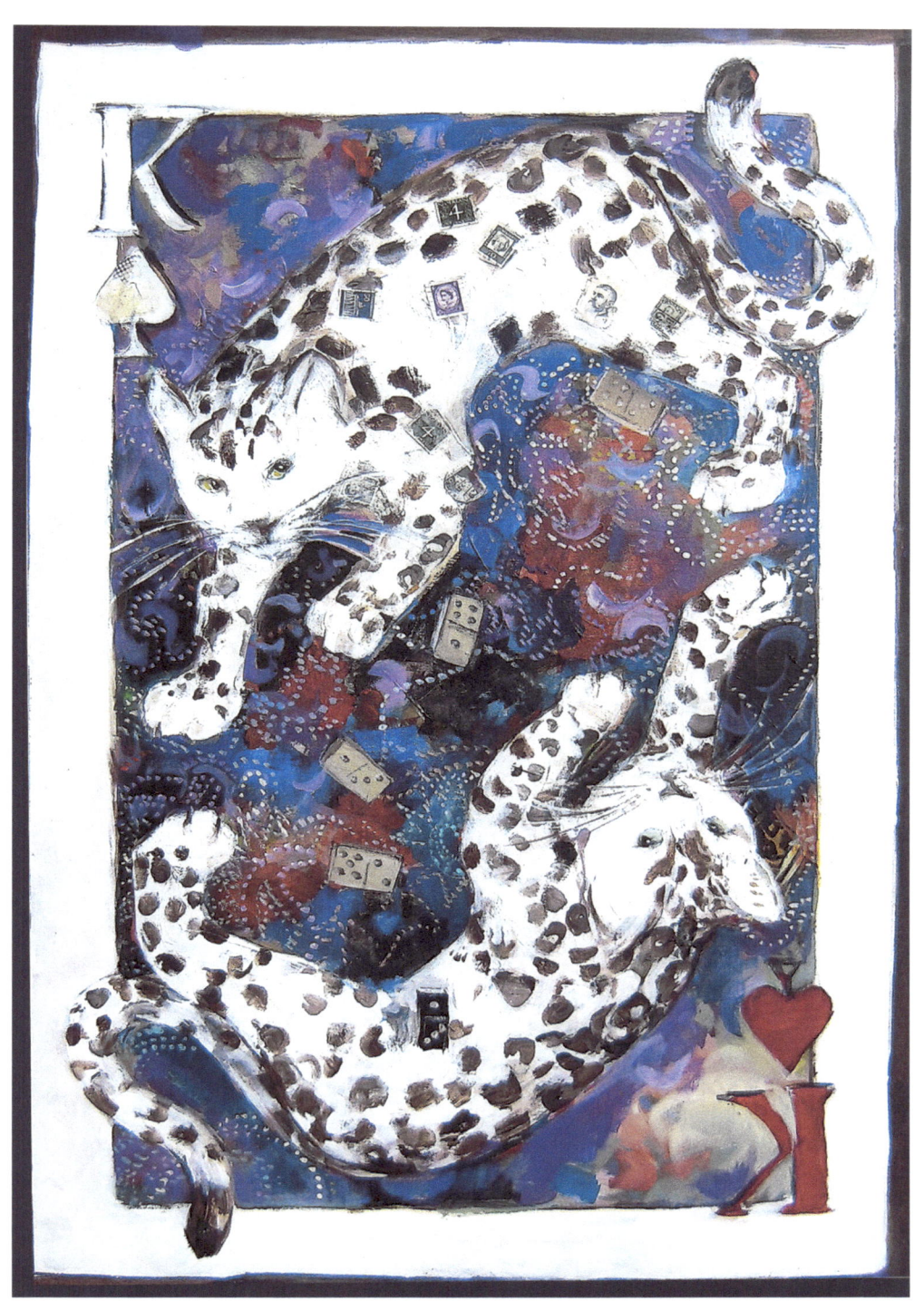

Turn Around
36"x24"

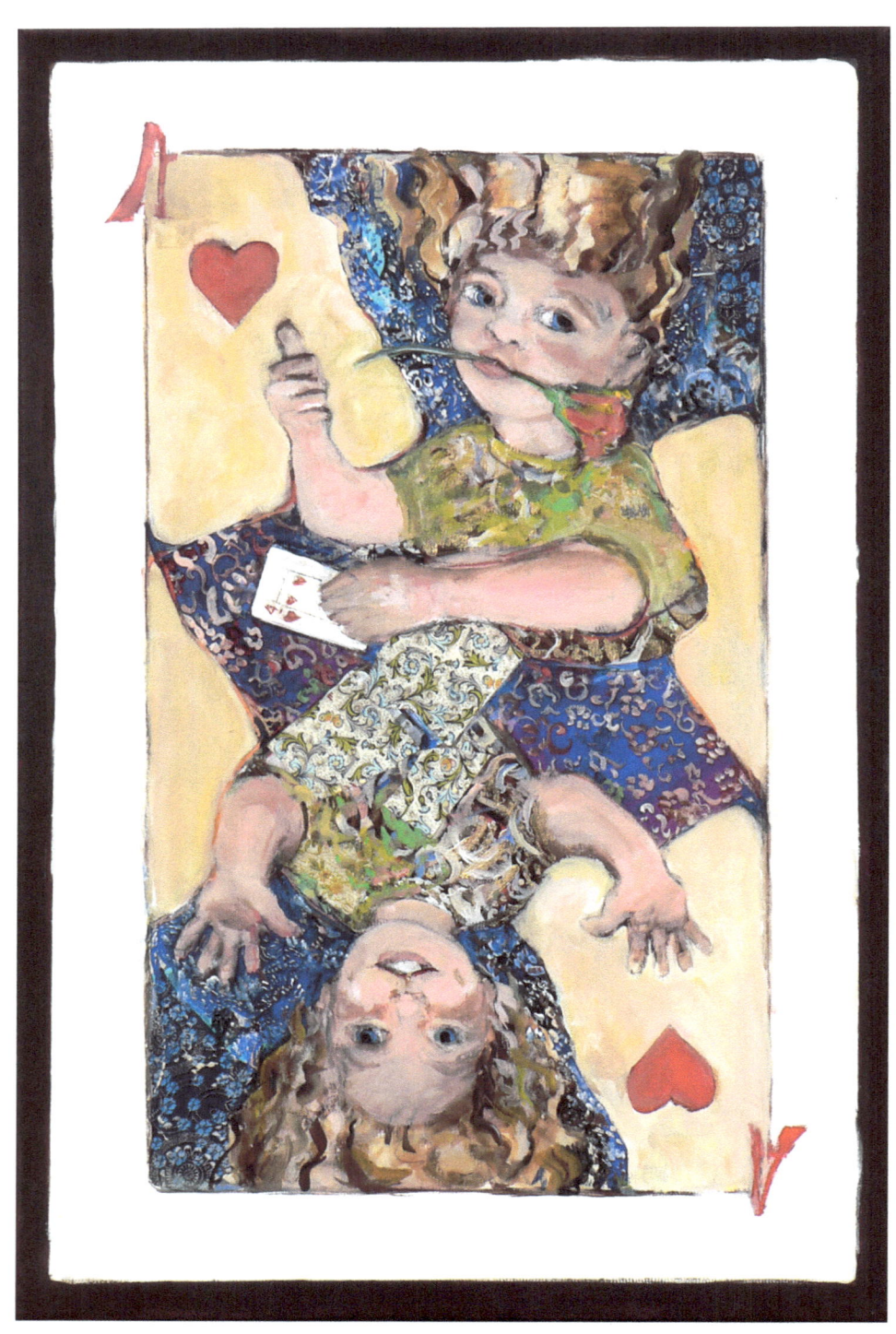

Ainsley at Four
30"x20"

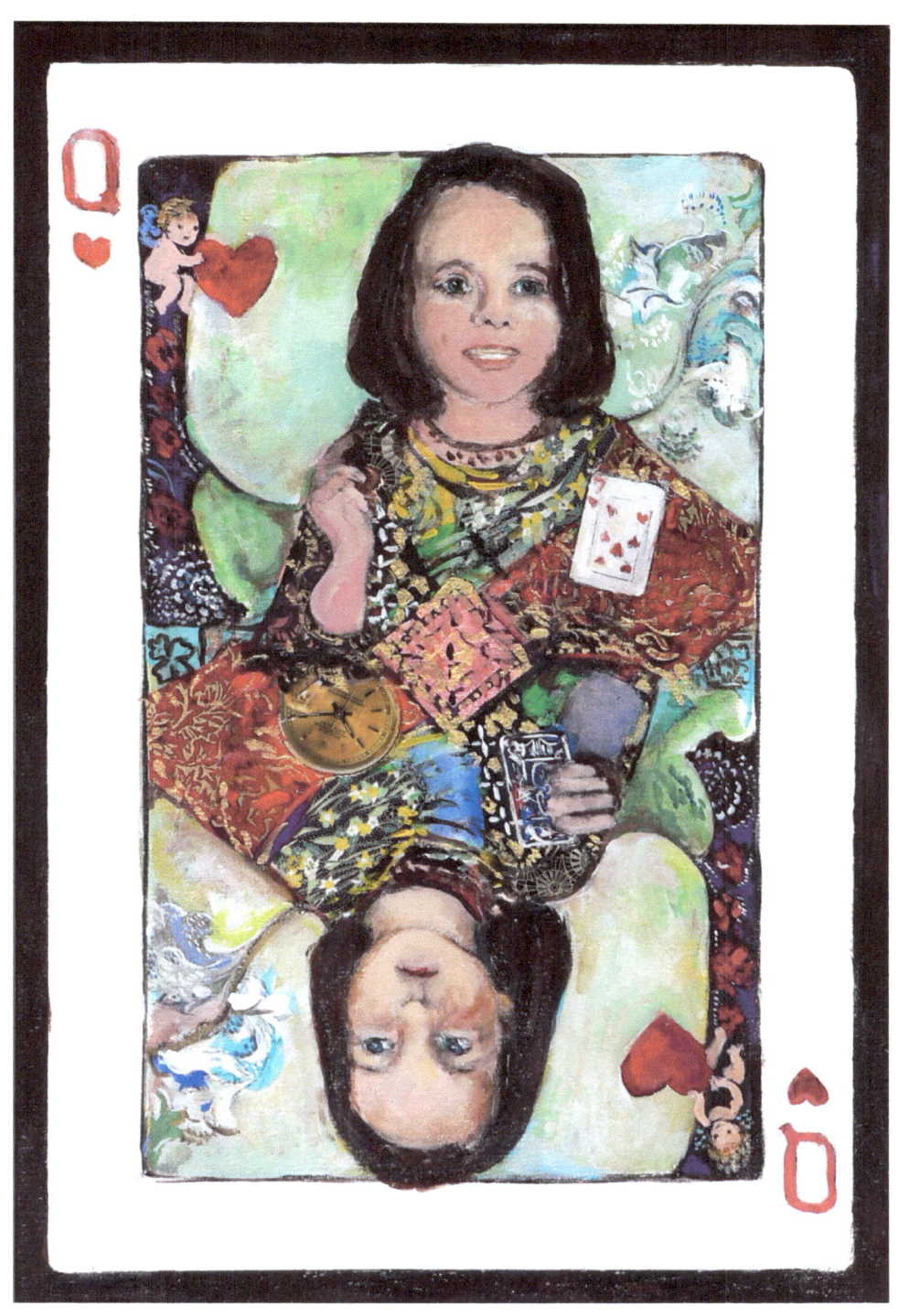

Hunter at Seven
30"x20"

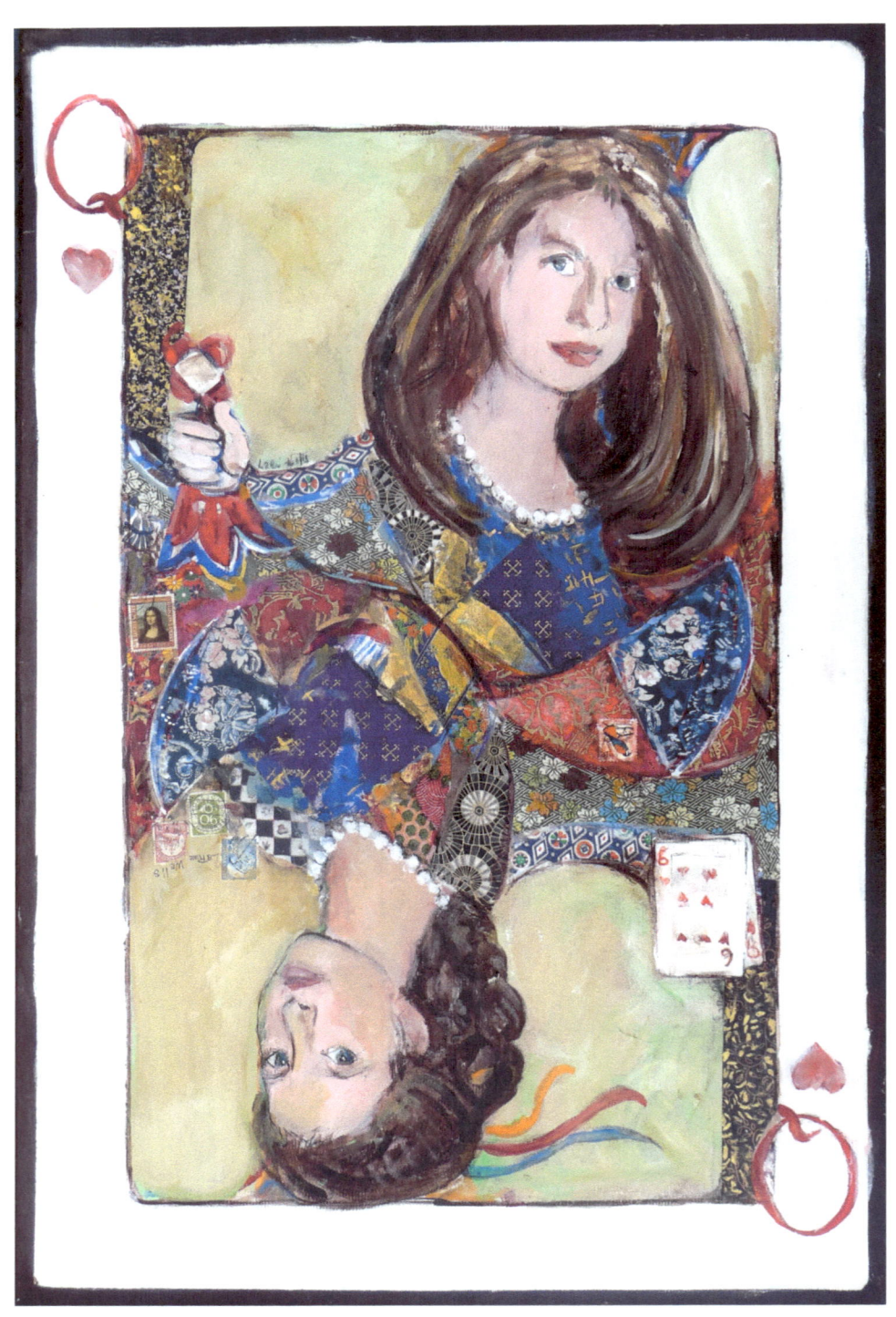

Carina at Fifteen
30"x20"

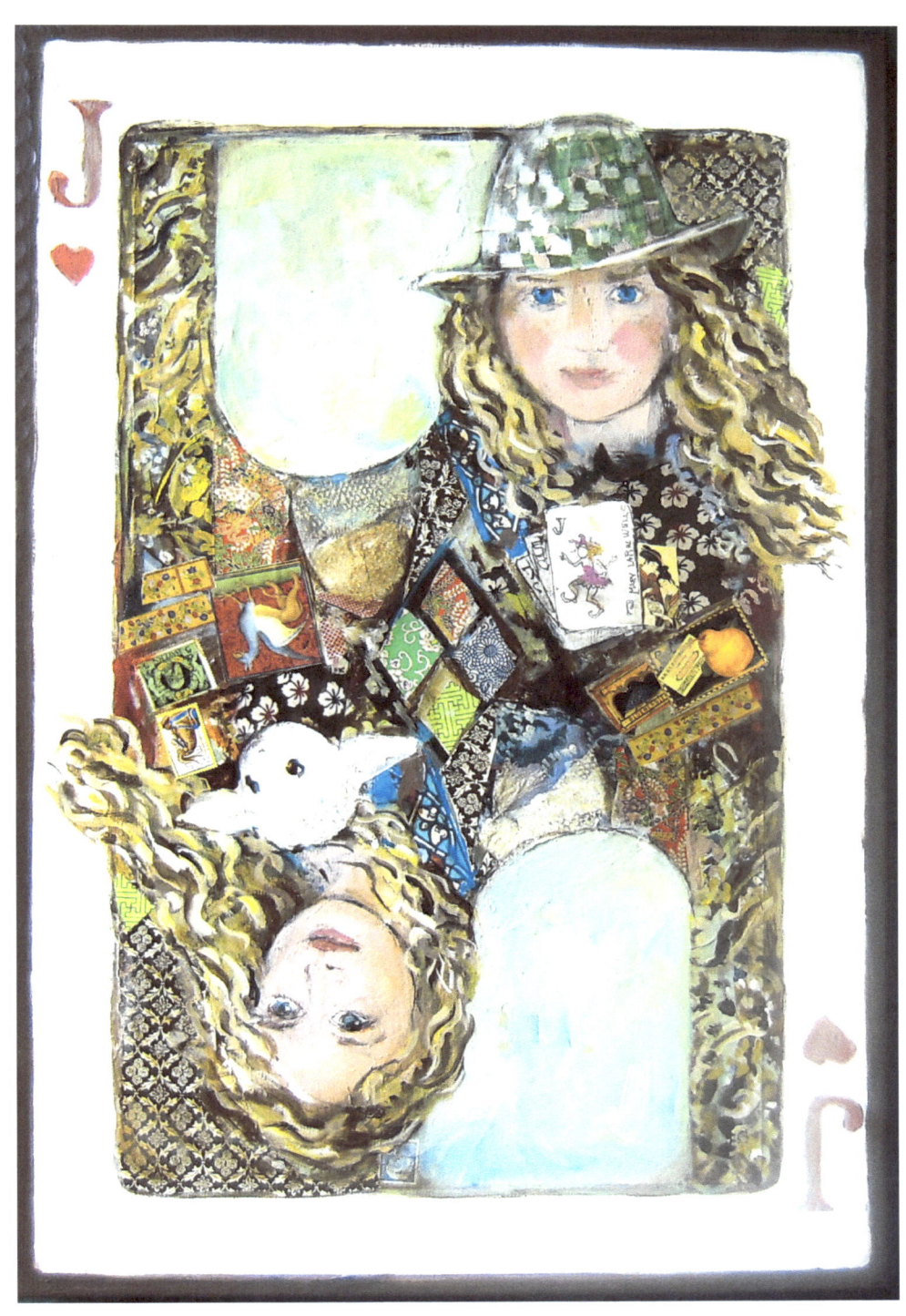

Maike at Twelve
30"x20"

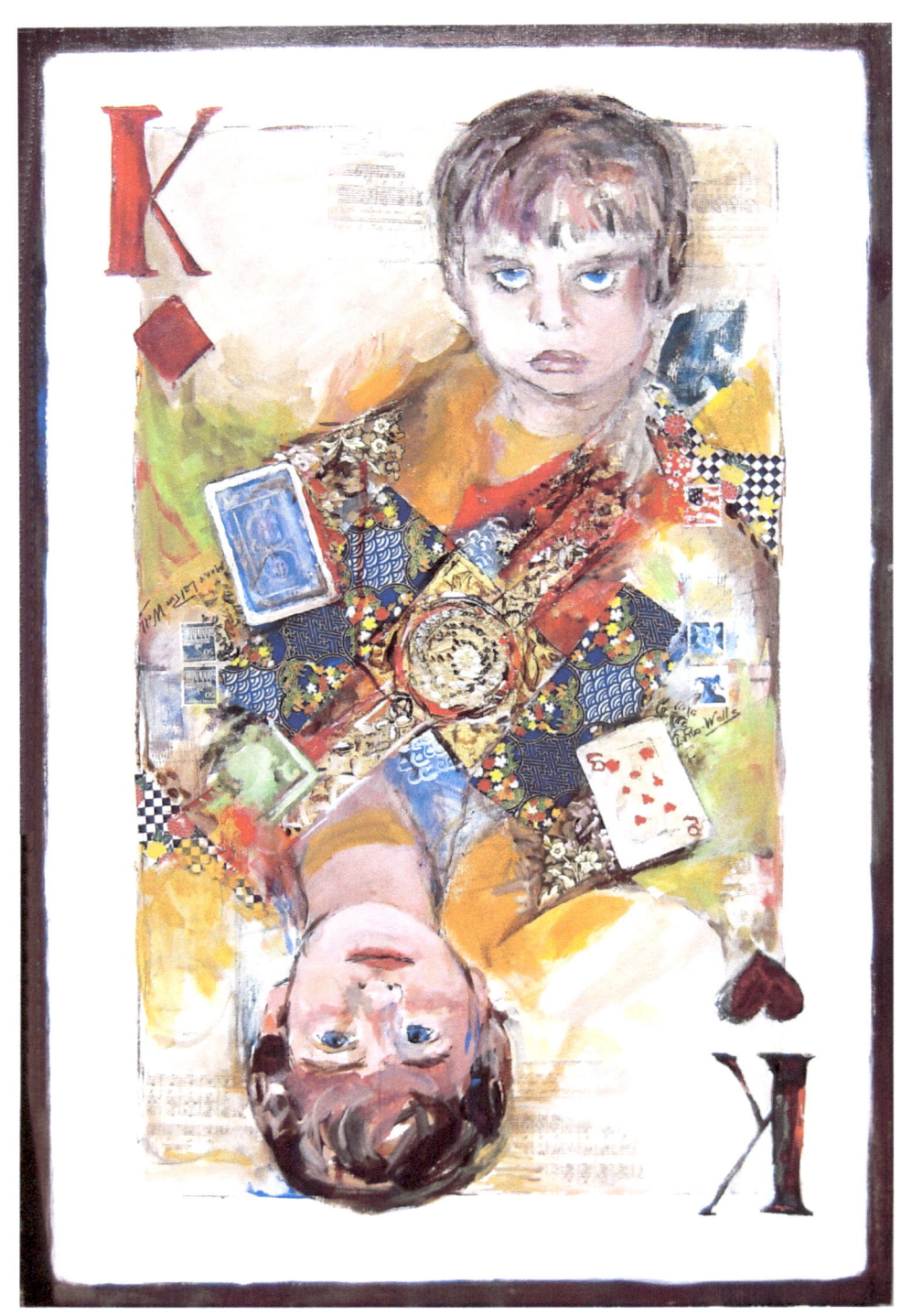

Christopher Gray at Nine
30"x20"

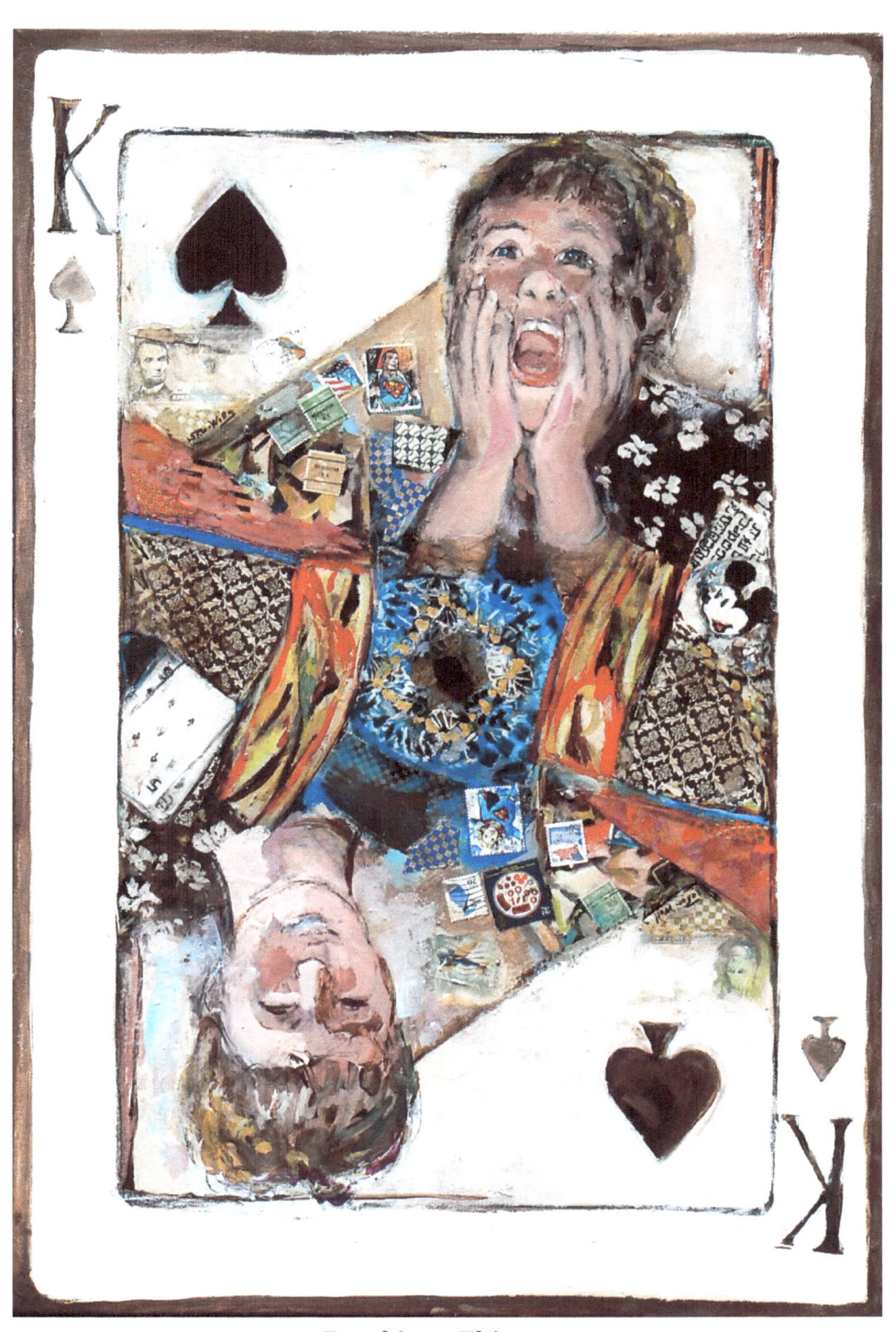

Frankie at Thirteen
30"x20"

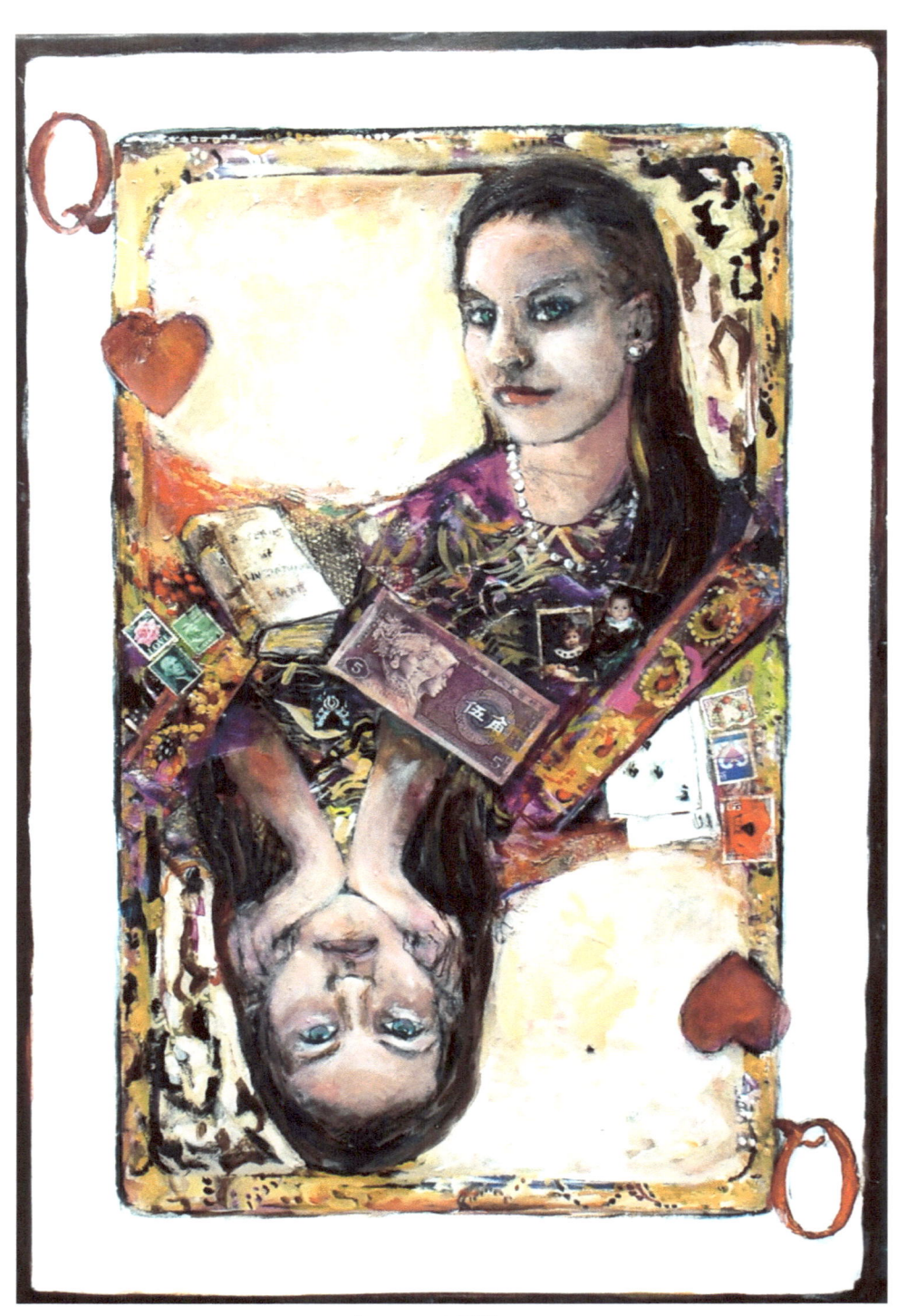

Jesse at Fifteen
30"x20"

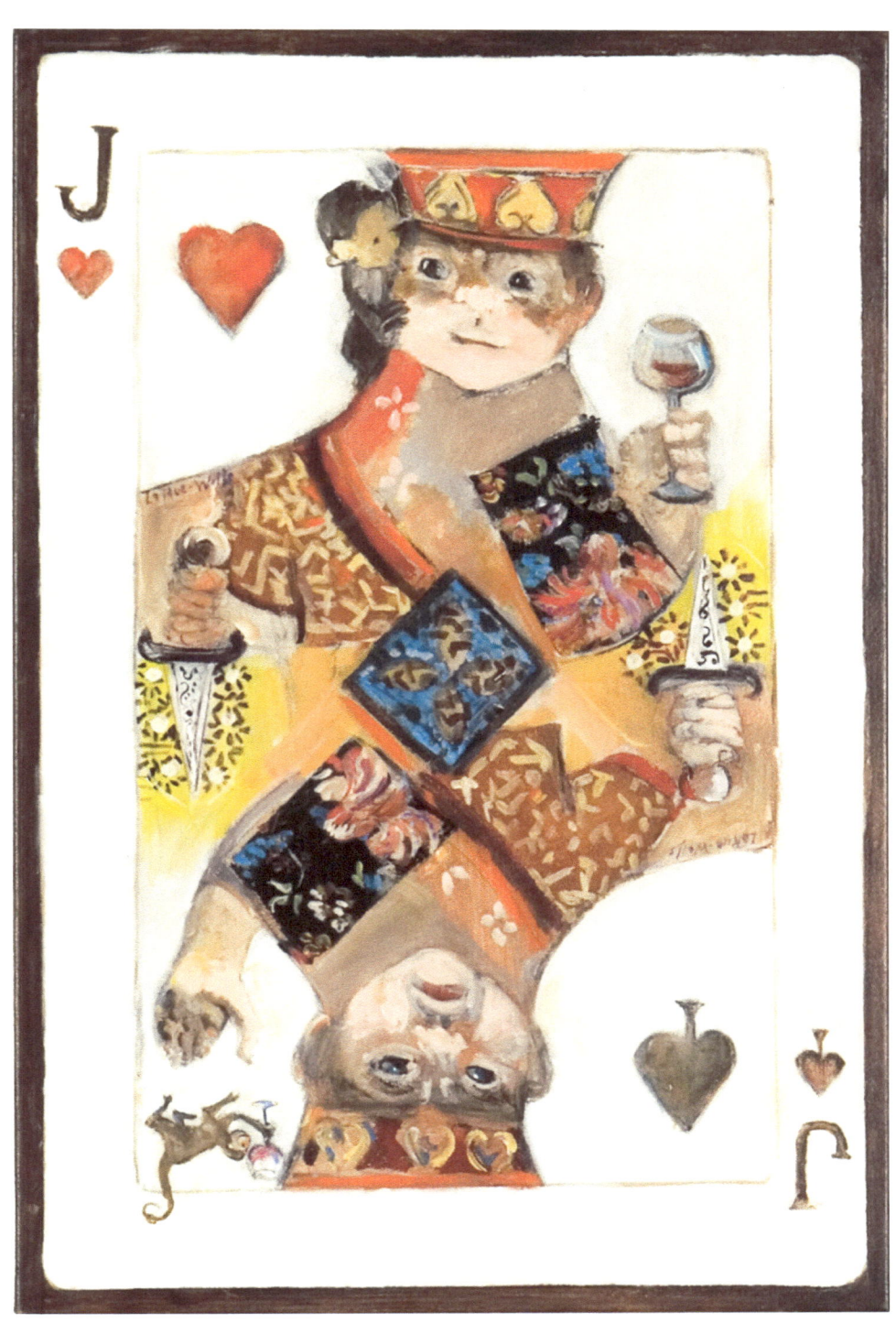

Monkey Business
30"x20"

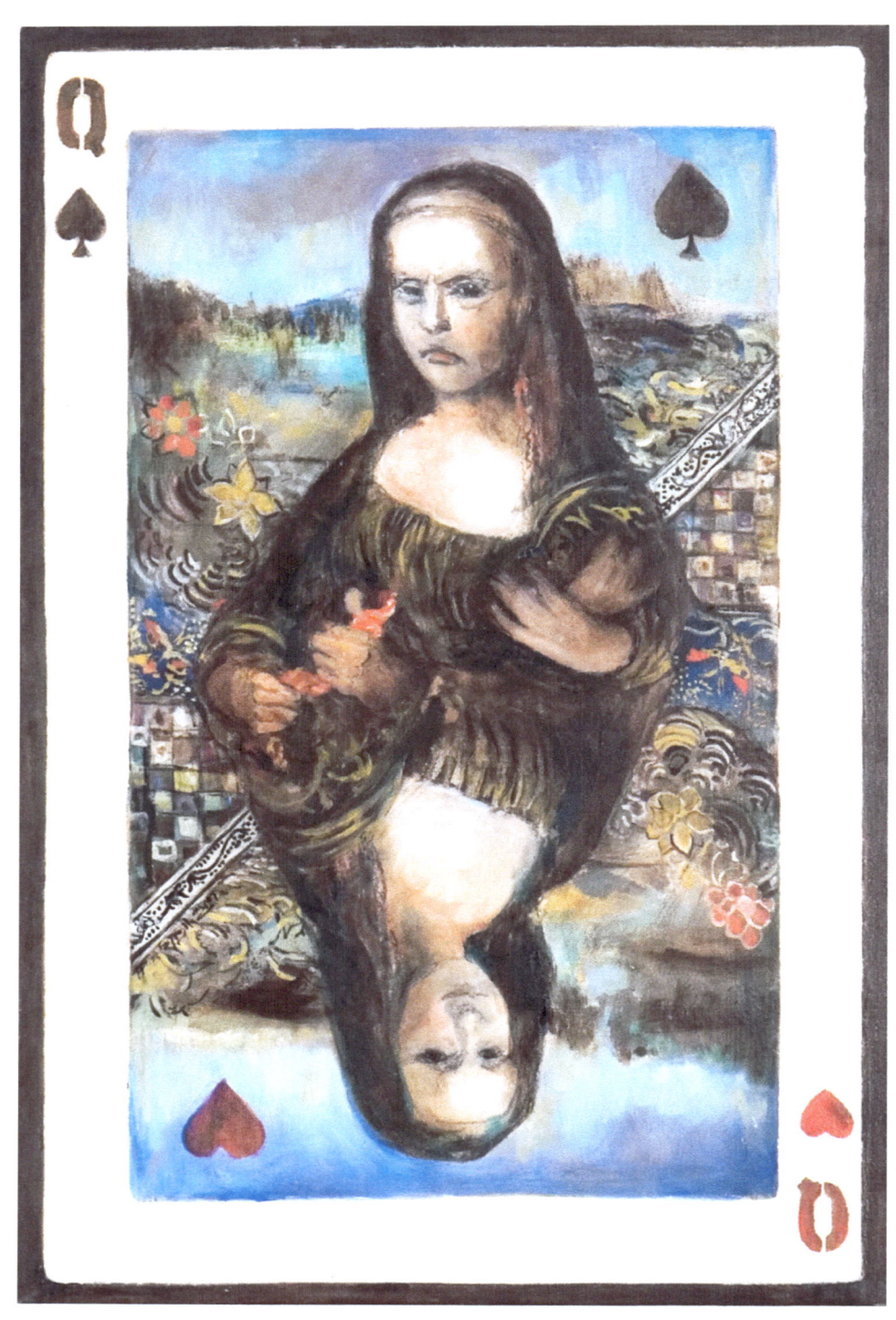

Some Times Mona Had a Bad Day
36"x24"

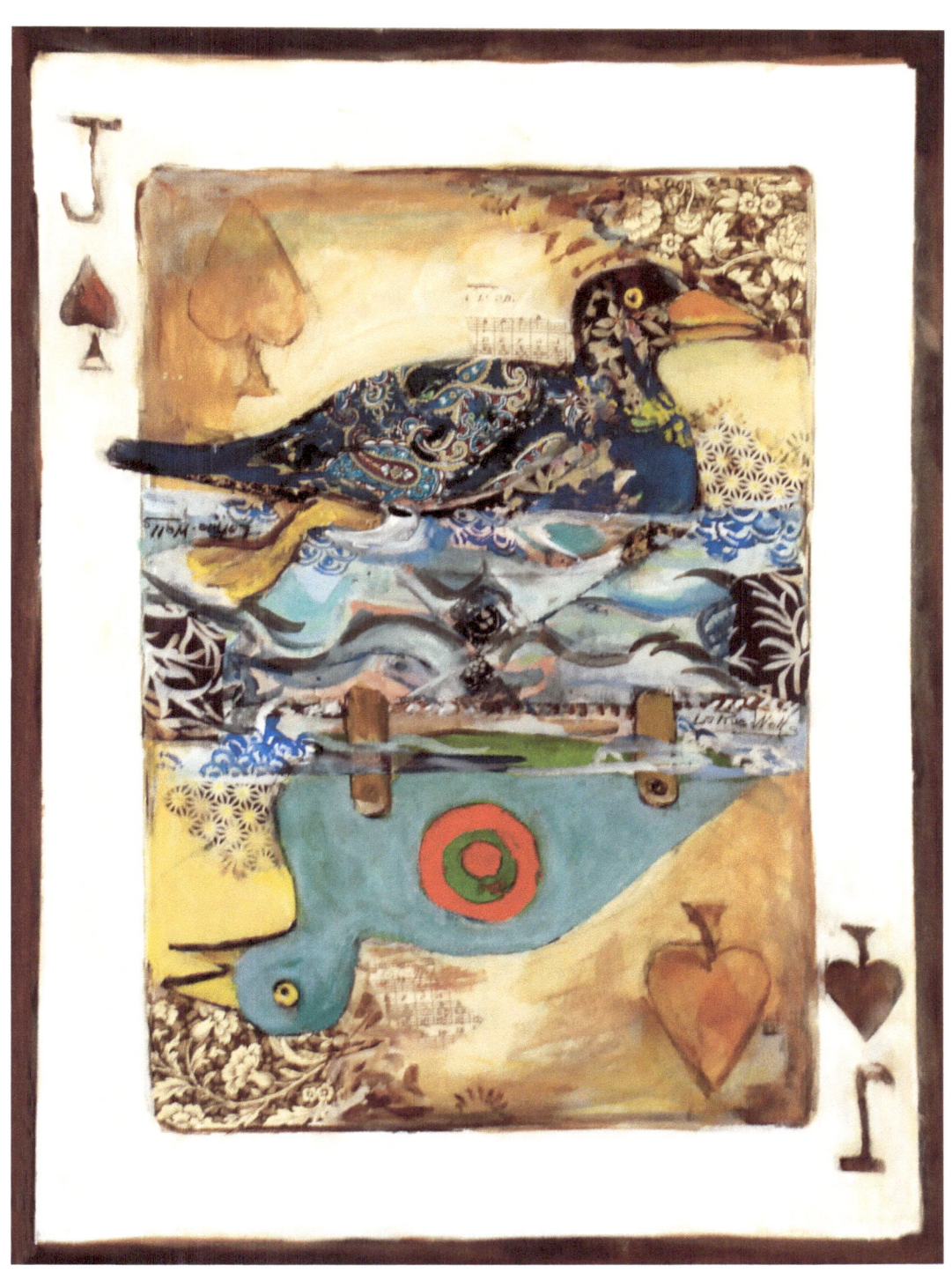

Target
24"x18"

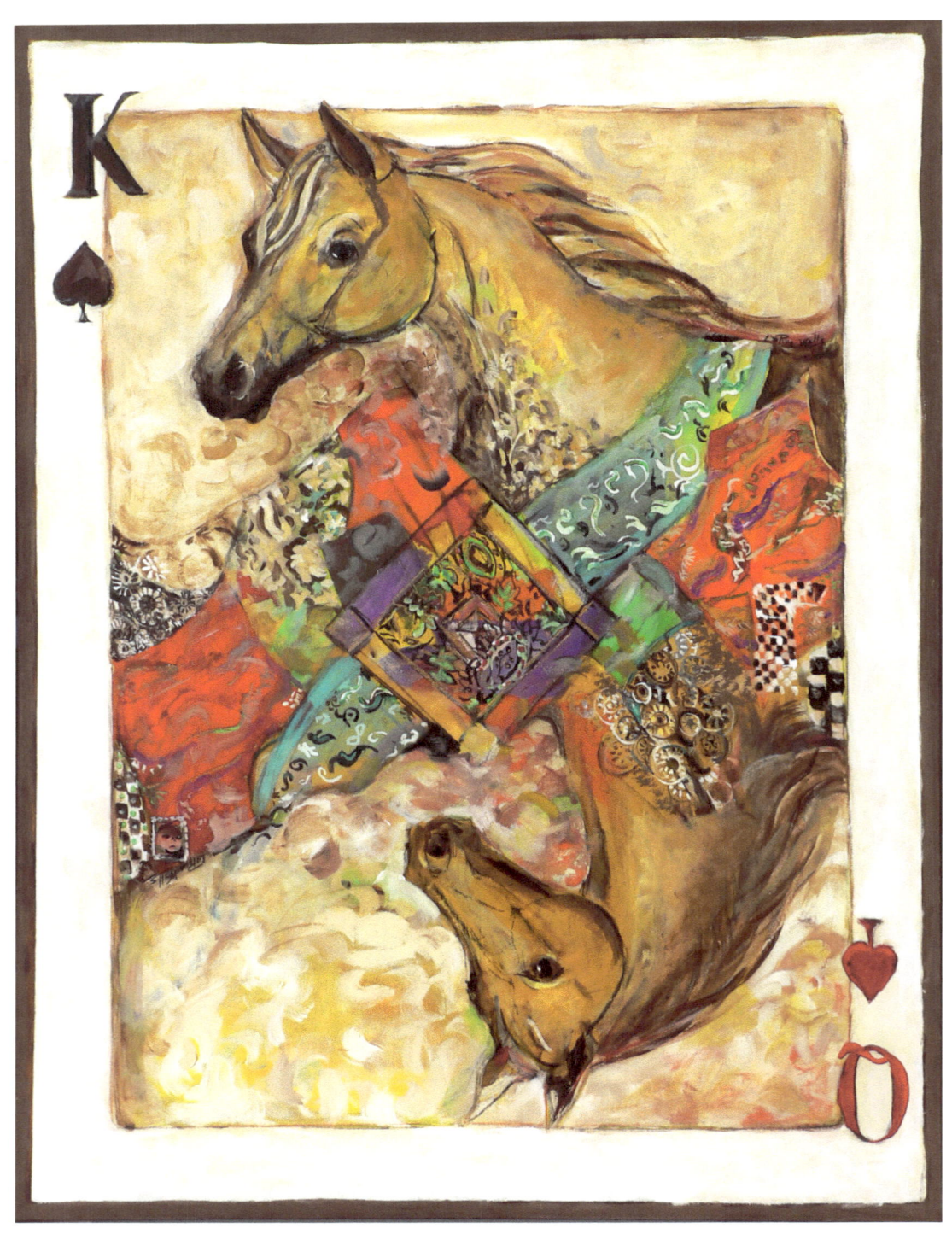

Horses
48"x36"

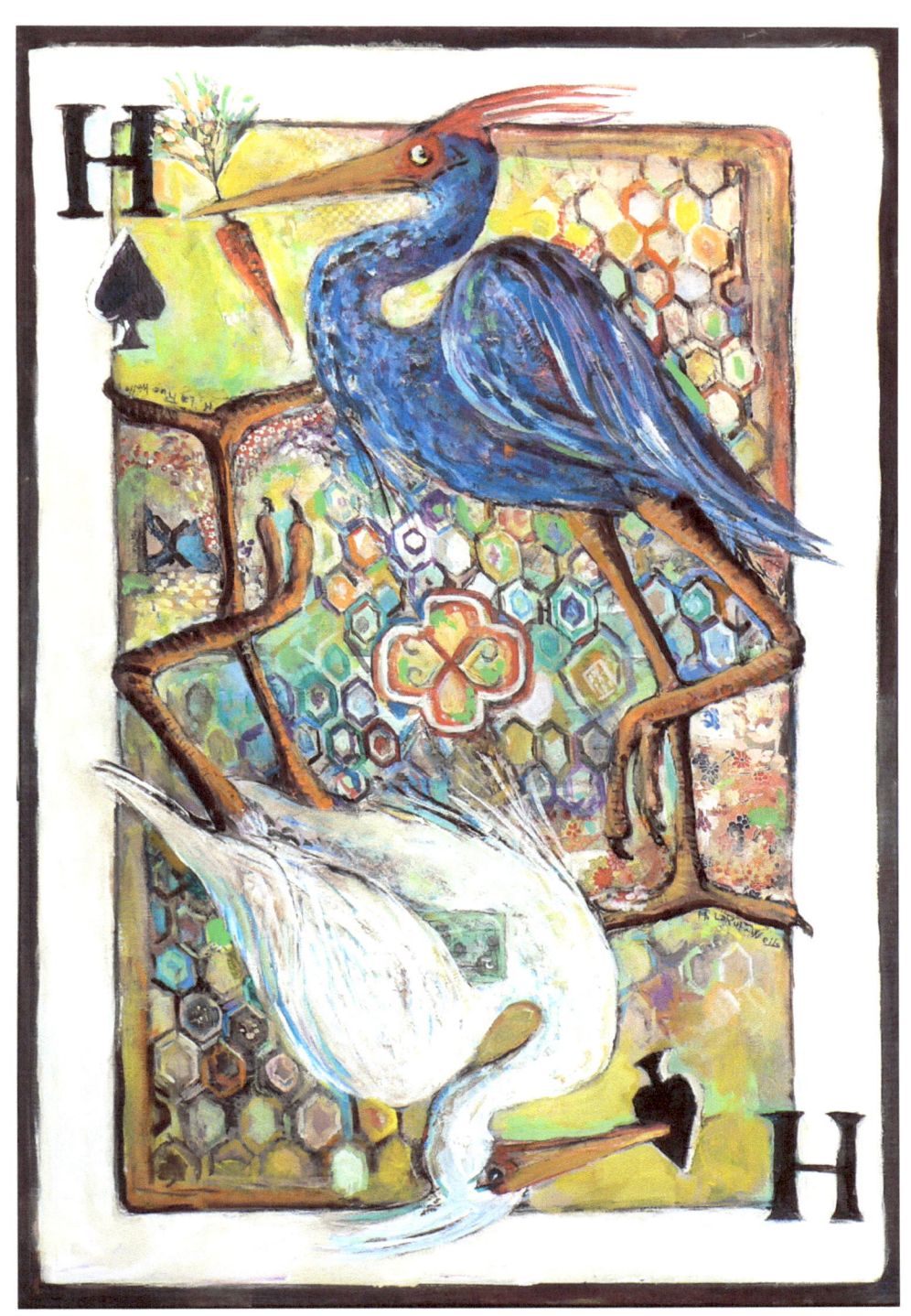

Herons
36"x24"

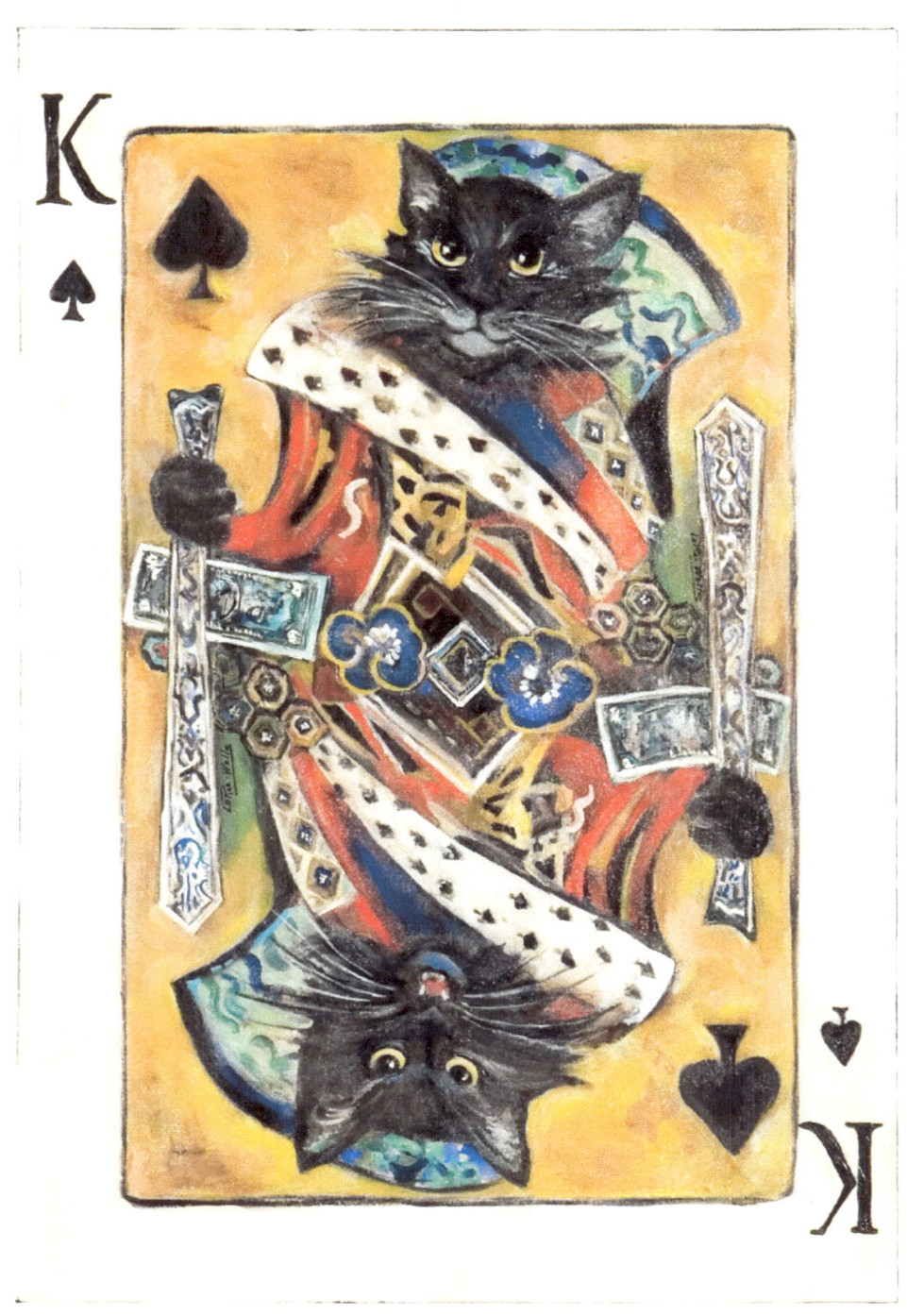

Deal or No Deal
36"x24"

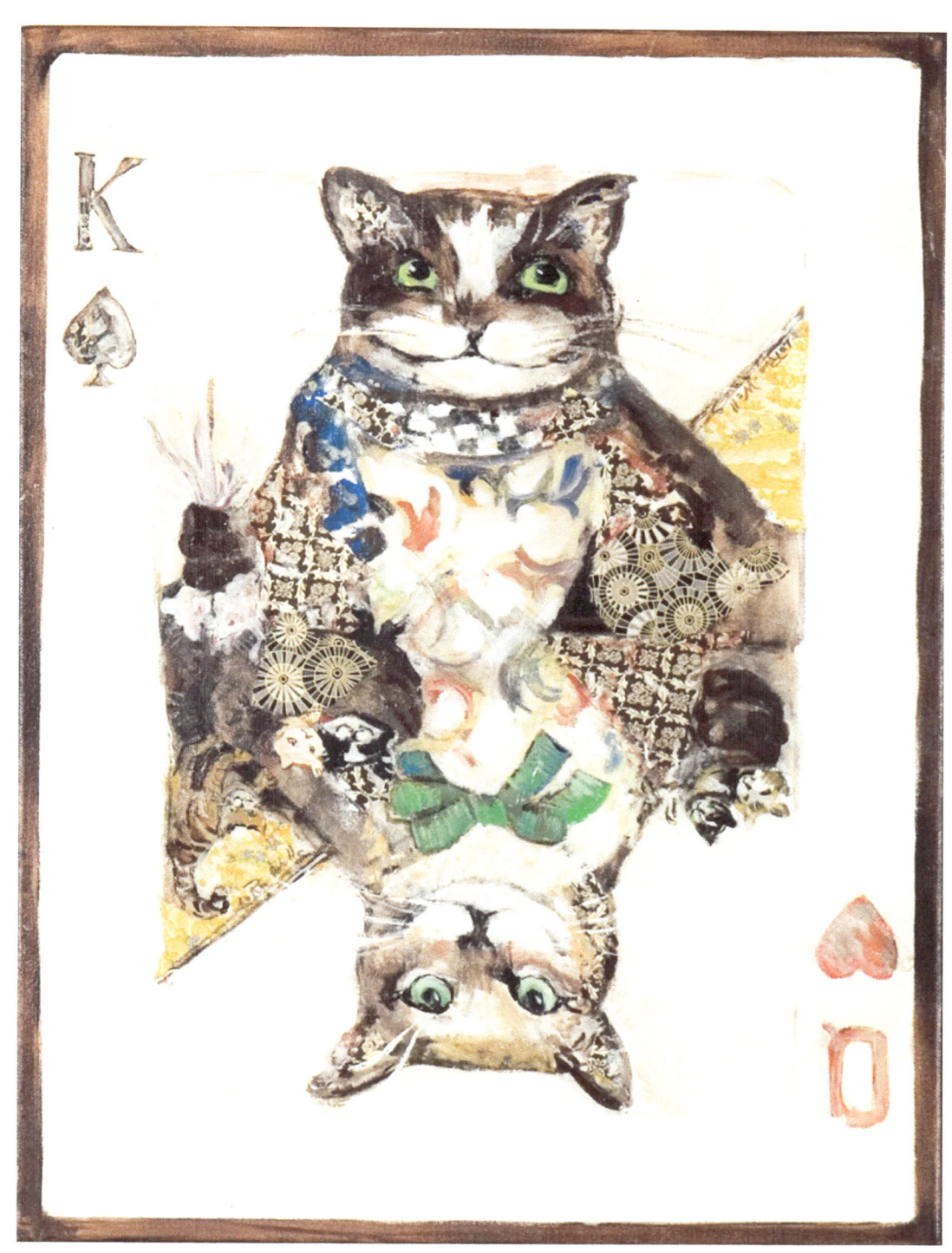

When Harry Met Sally
24"x18"

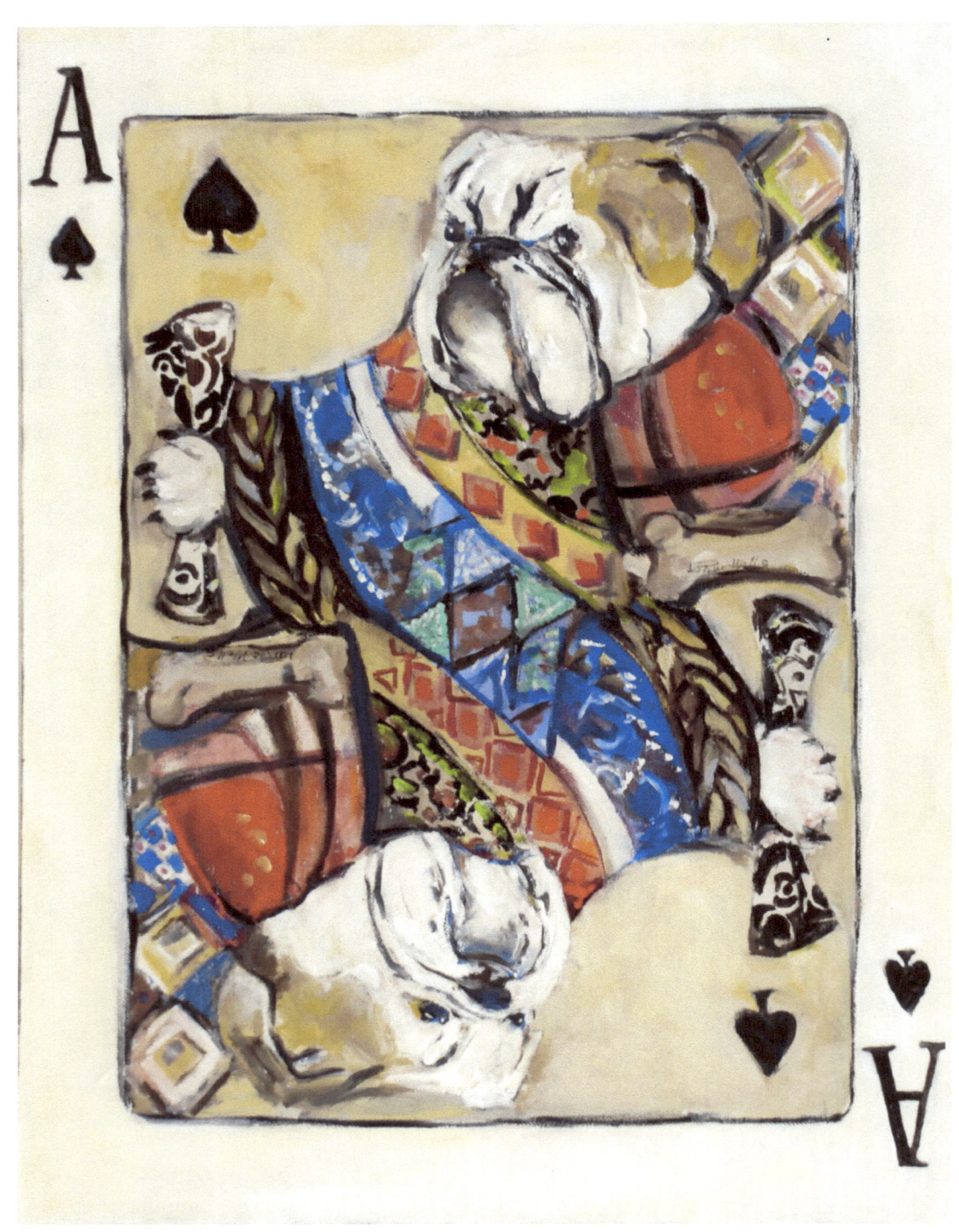

Dan's Dog
20"x16"

CATS

My cat series shows us all the intelligence, beauty, and often mischievous nature of our always surprising feline companions.

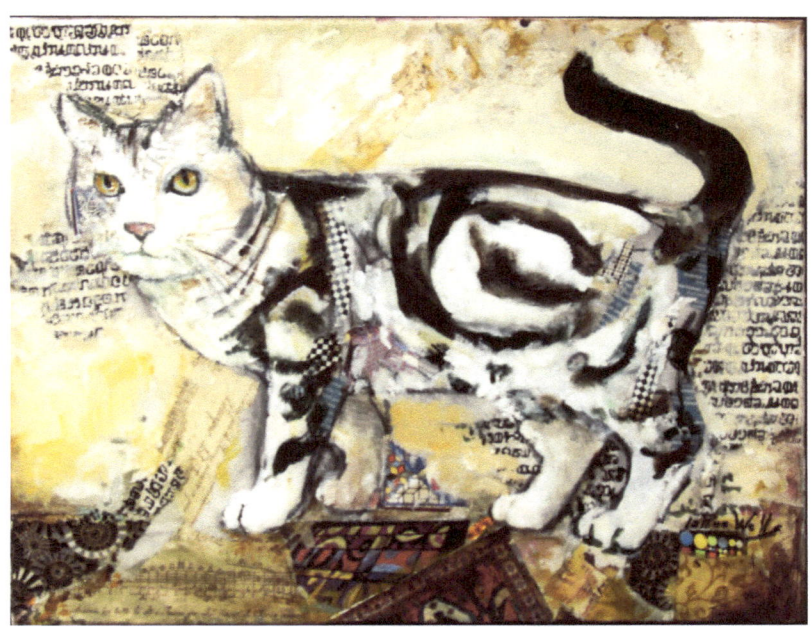

Literary Cat
14"x18"

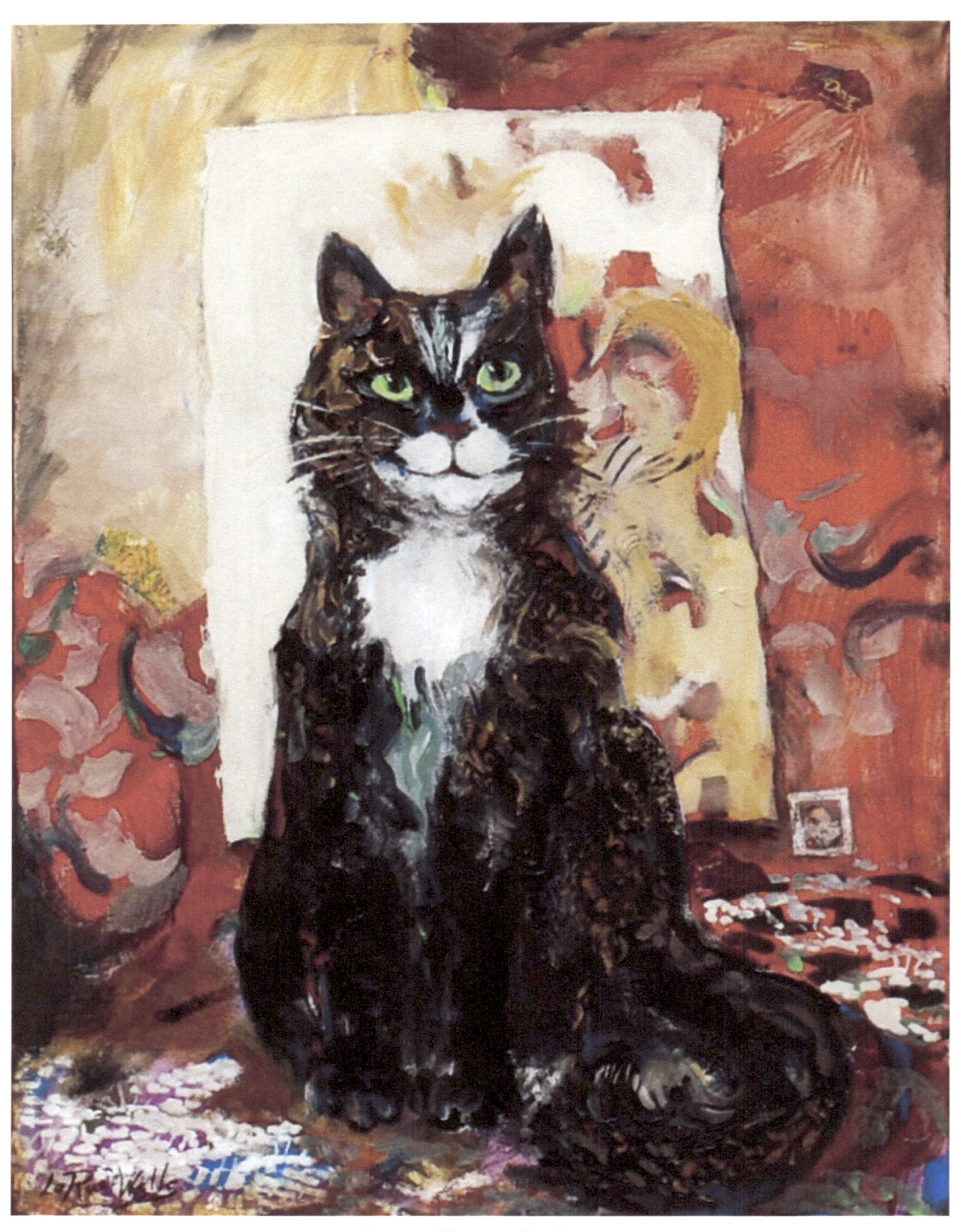

The Well Satisfied Cat
24"x18"

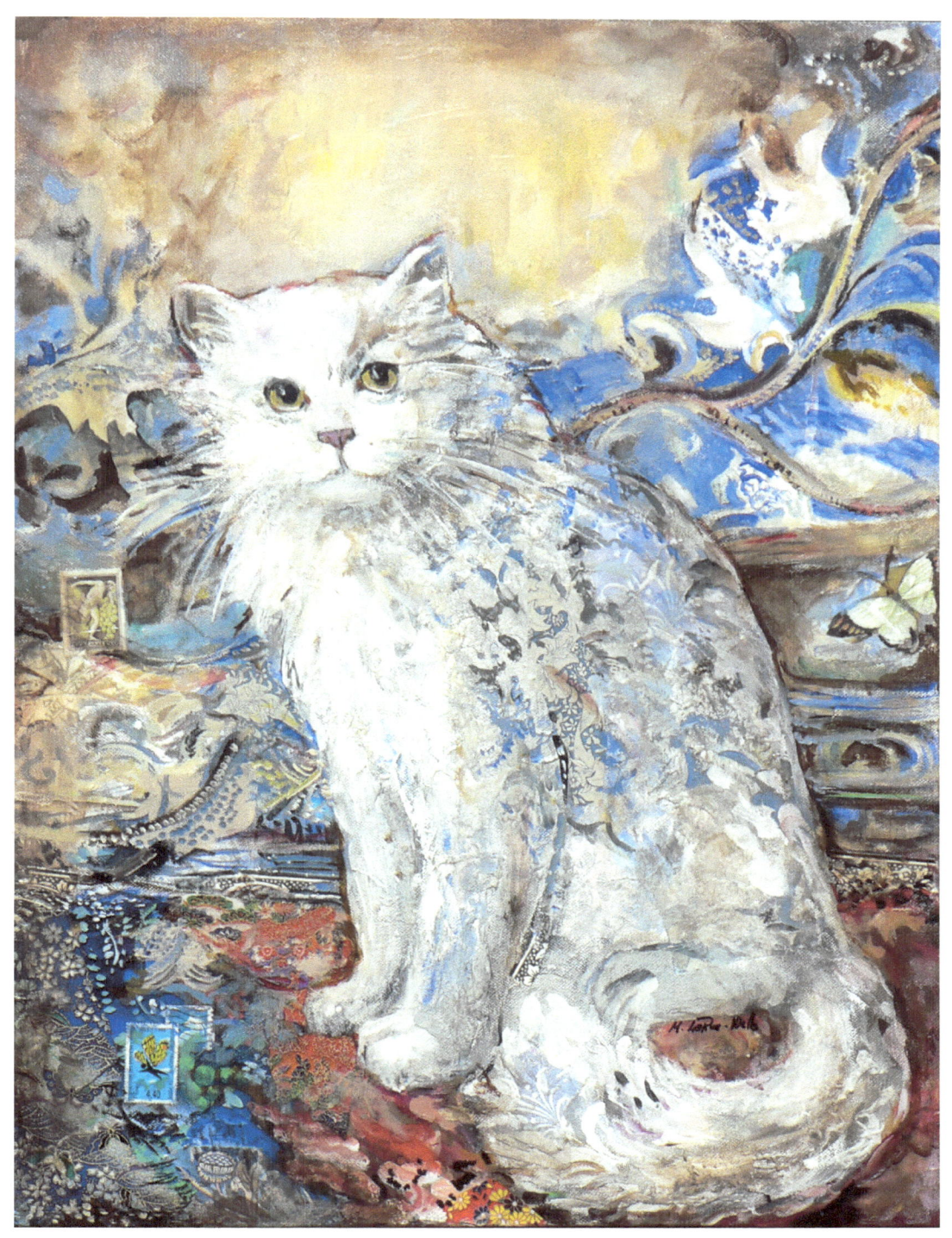

Sophisticat
24"x18"

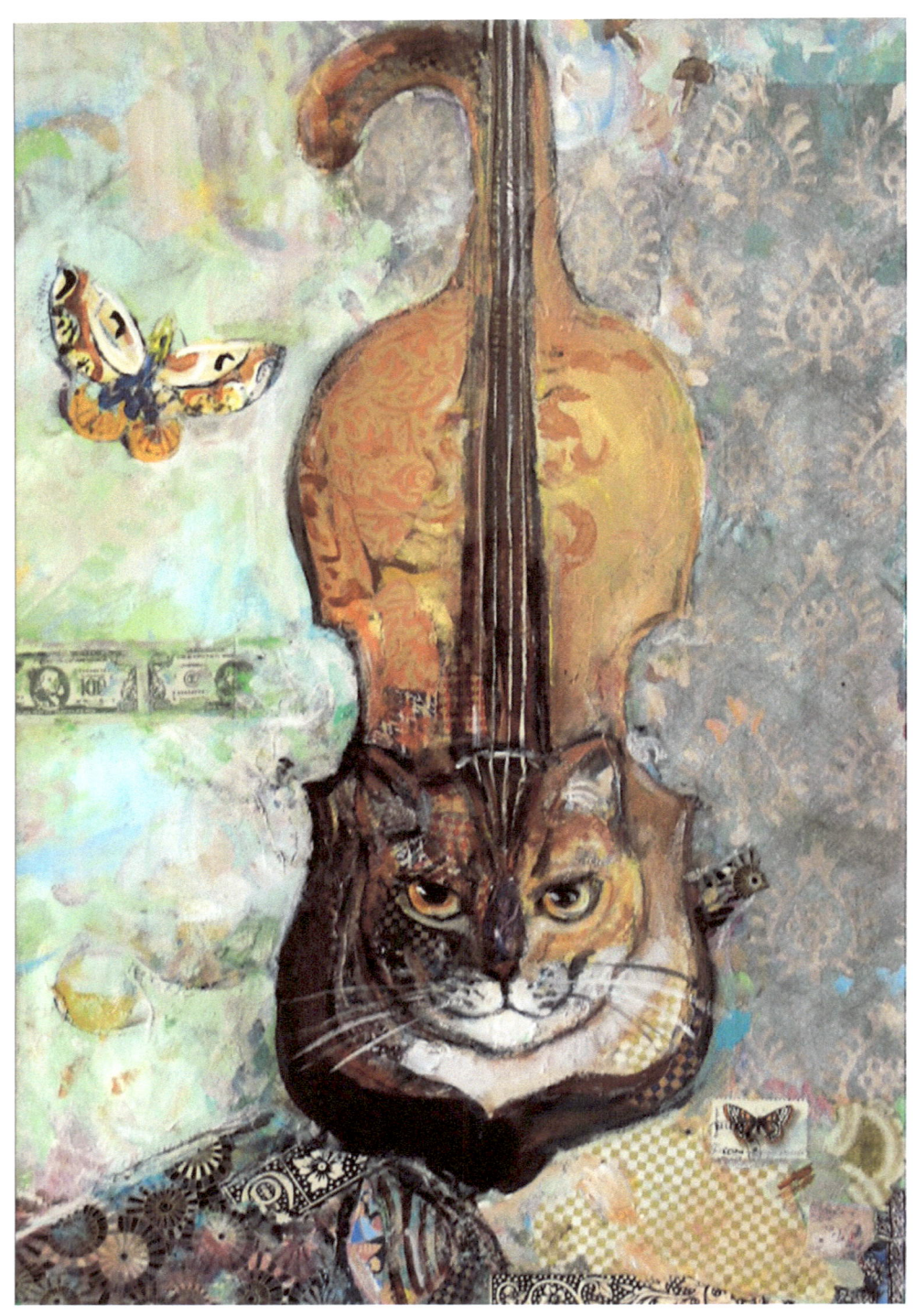

Violin Cat #3
22"x15"

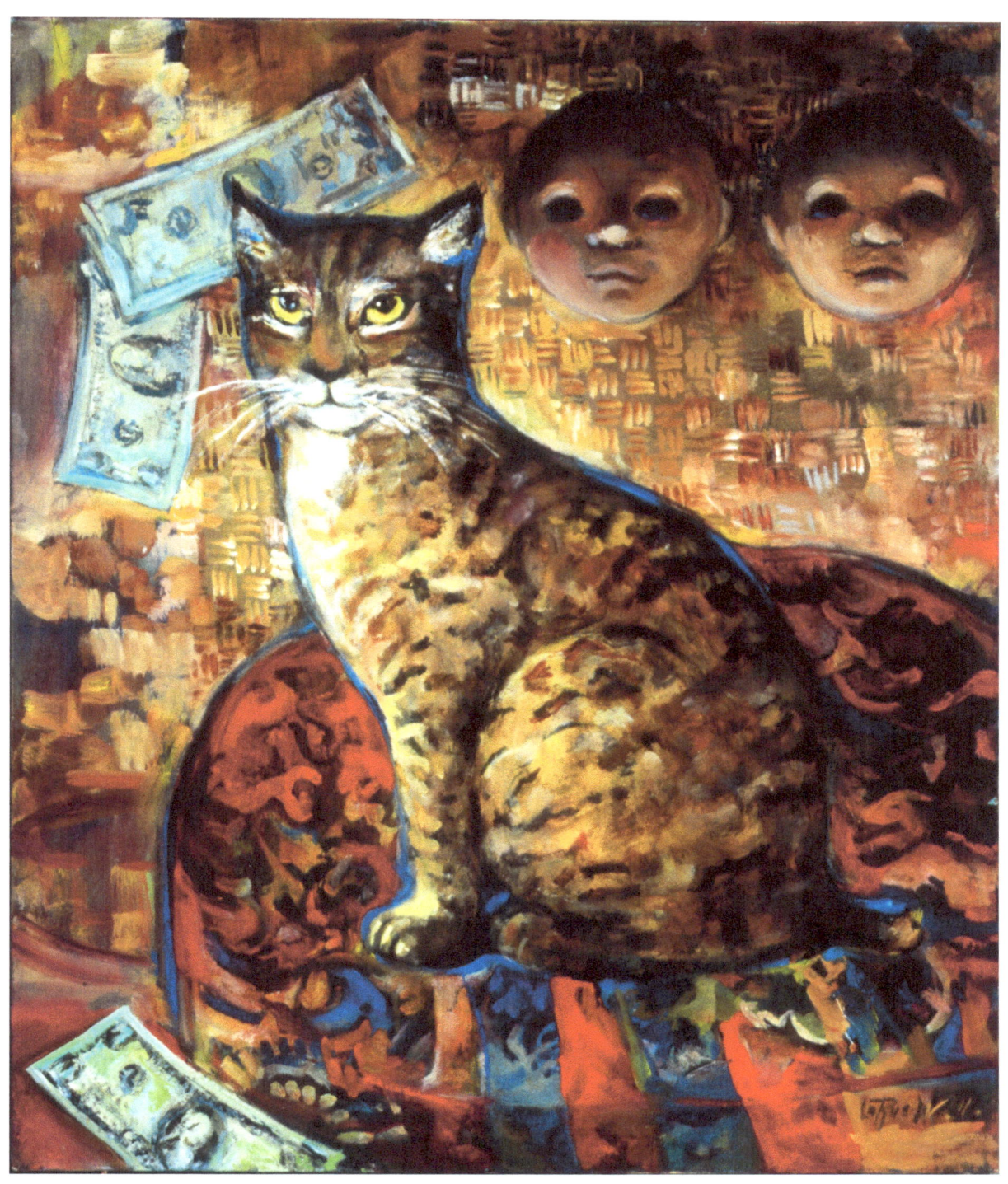

Mysterious Cat
30"x24"

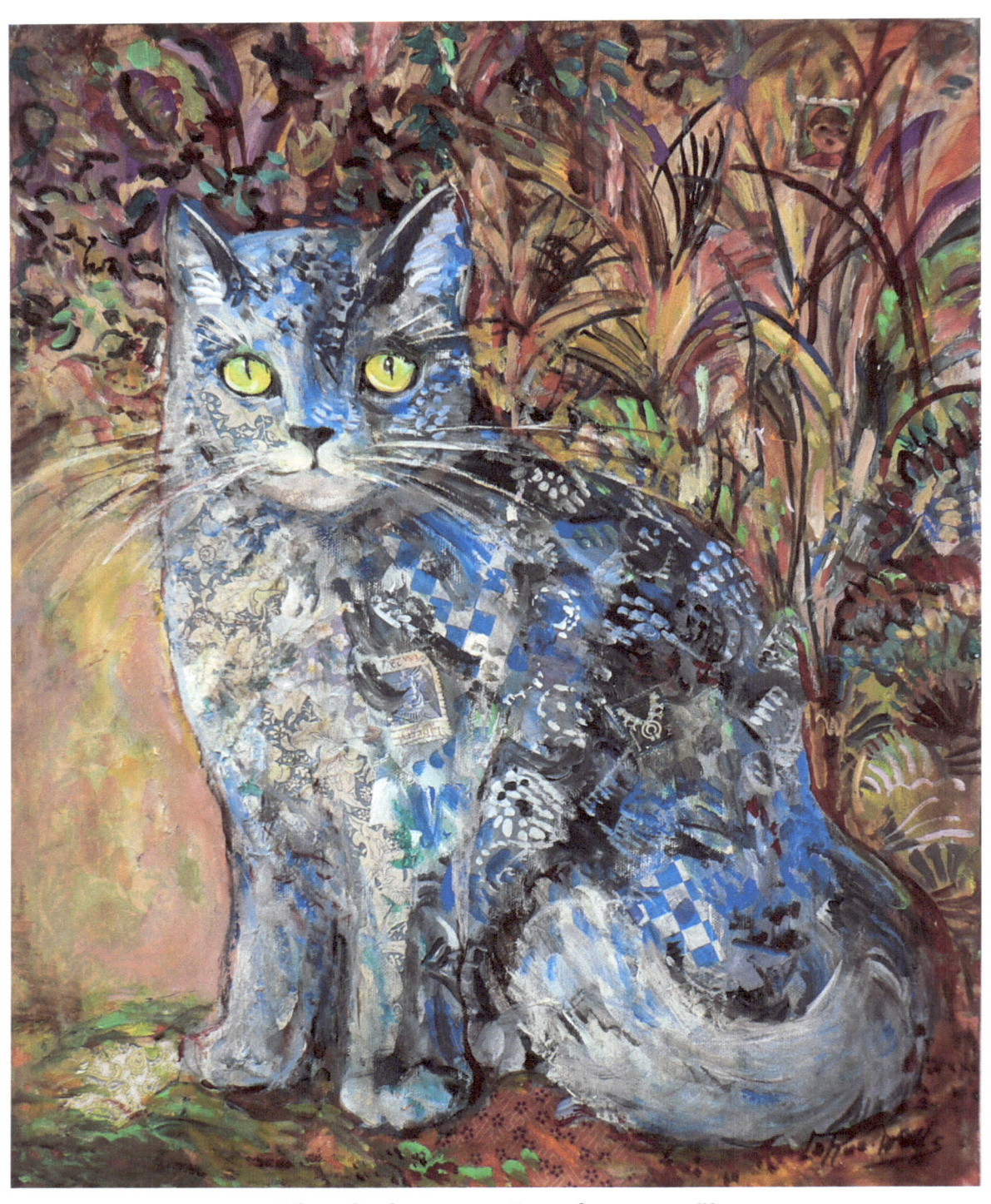

What do they mean "put the cat out"?
20"x16"

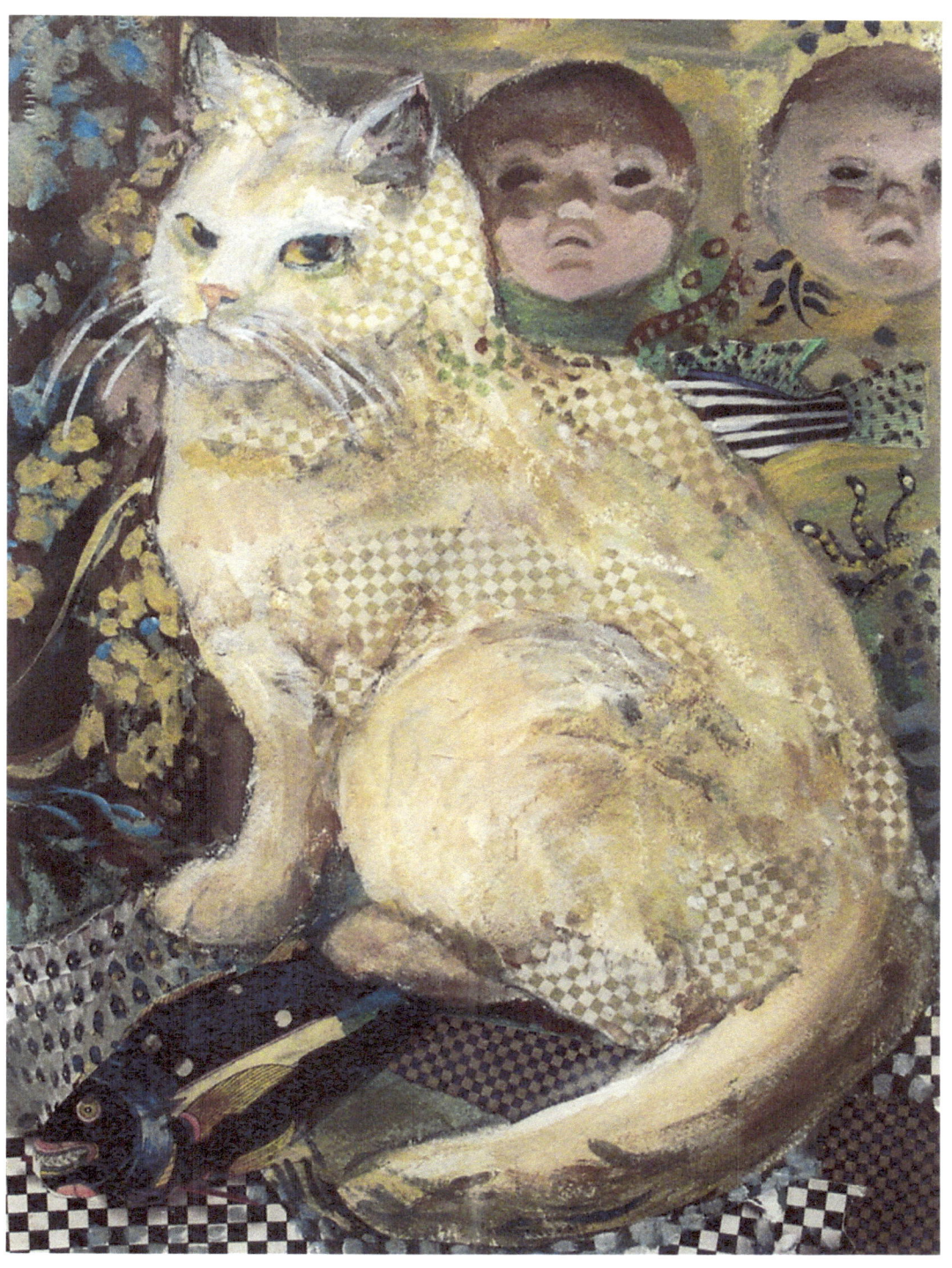

Chester
15"x11"

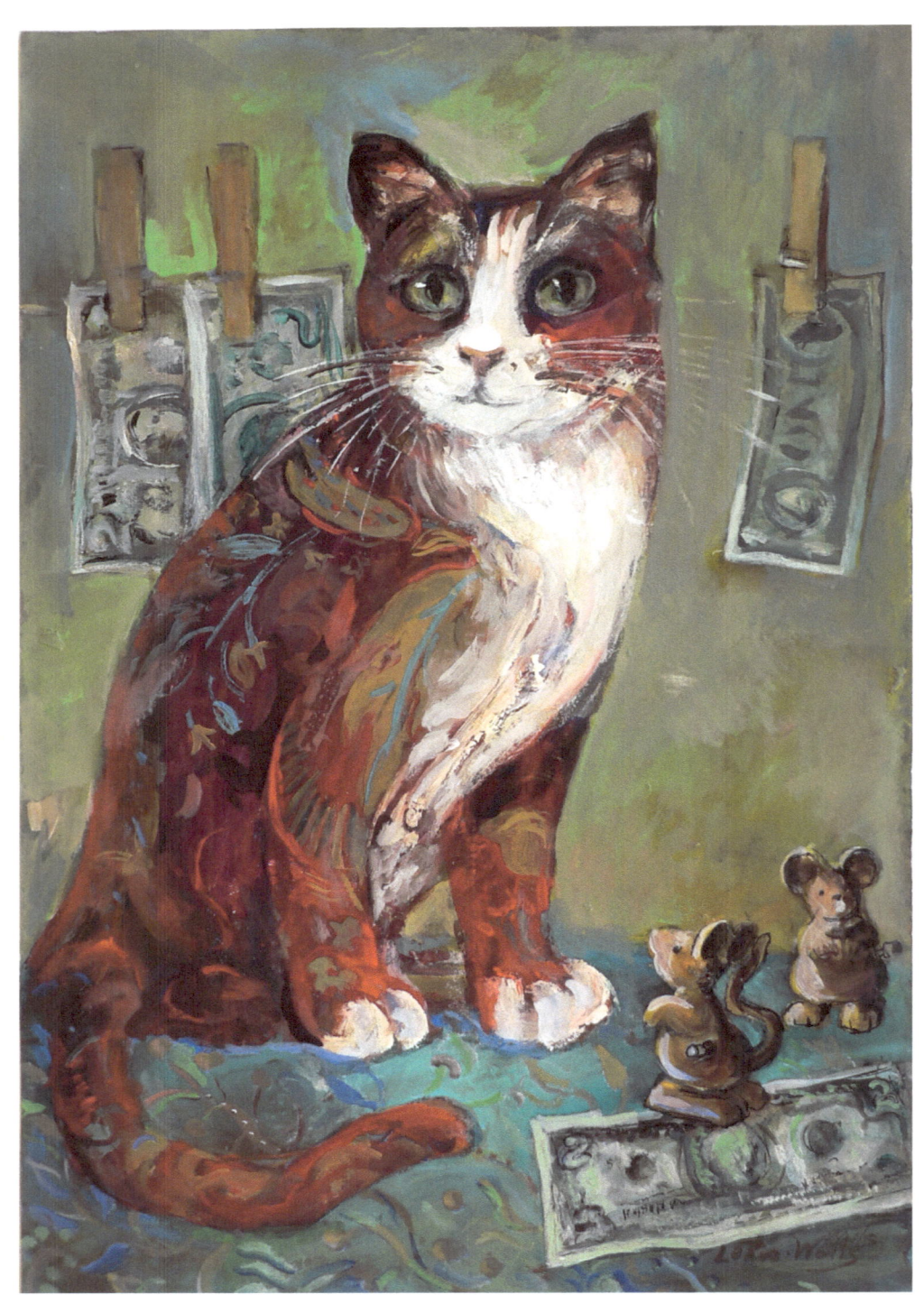

Hanging Out
20"x13"

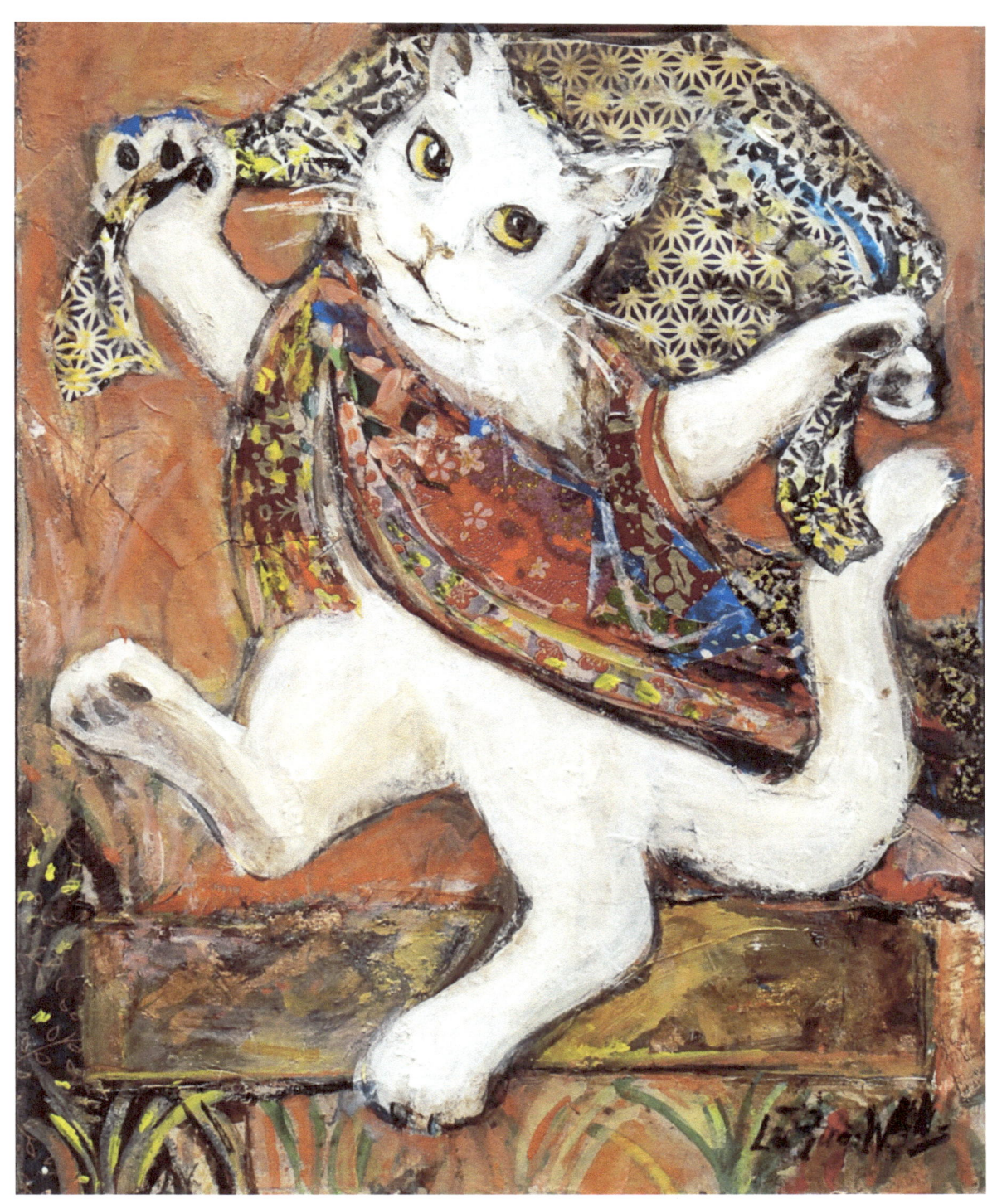

Miss Molly the Go-Go Girl
14"x11"

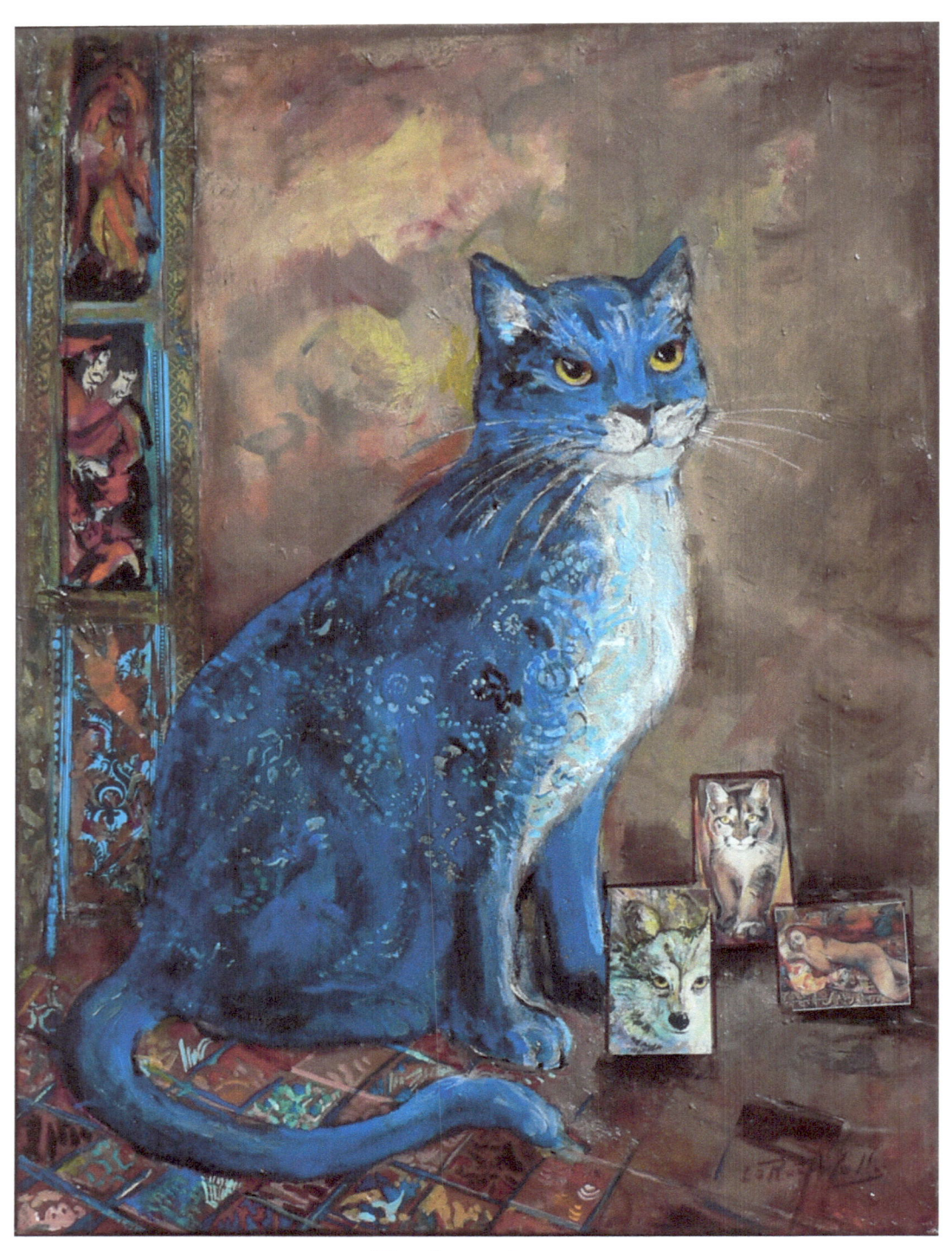

The Connoisseur
24"x18"

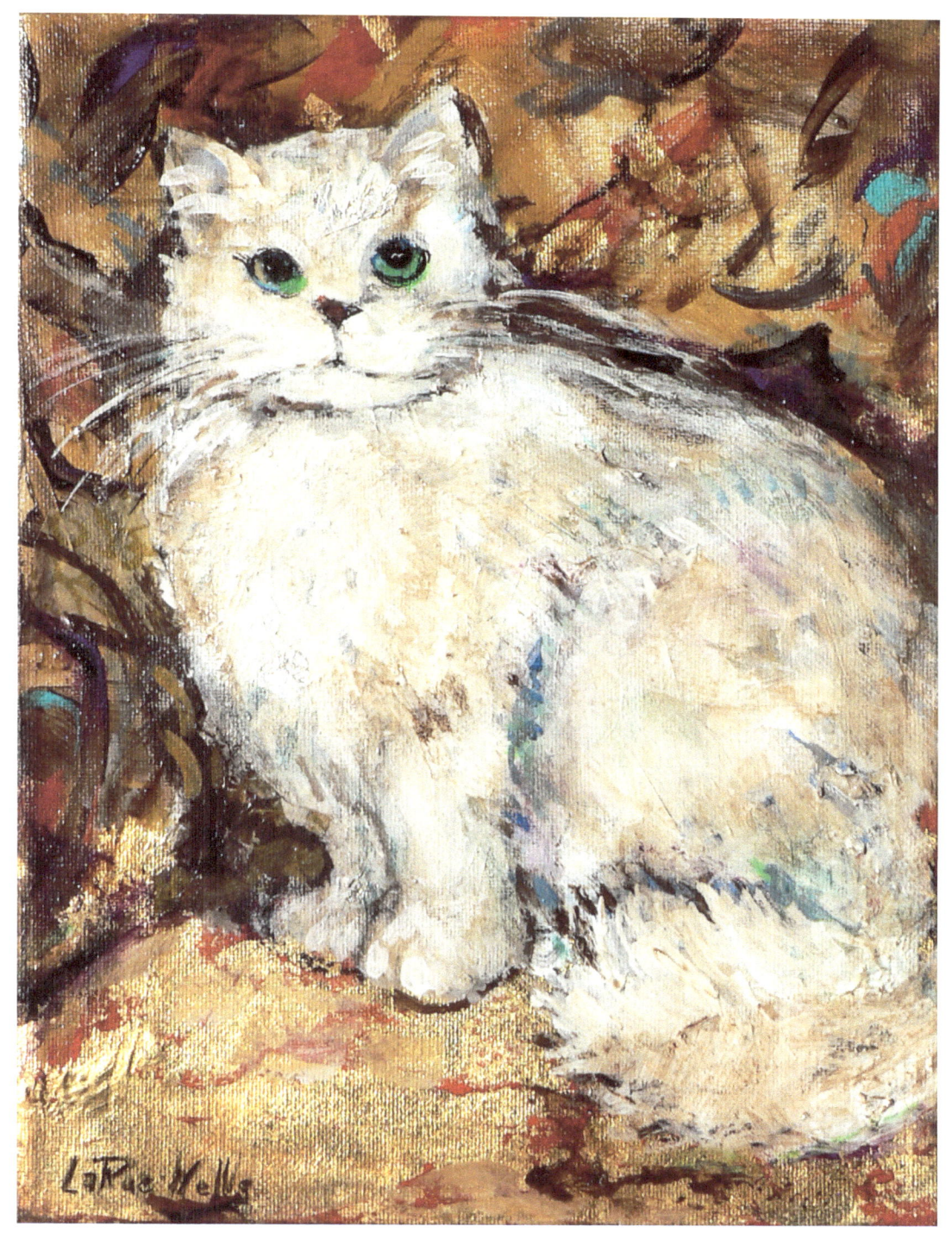

Green Eyes
12"x9"

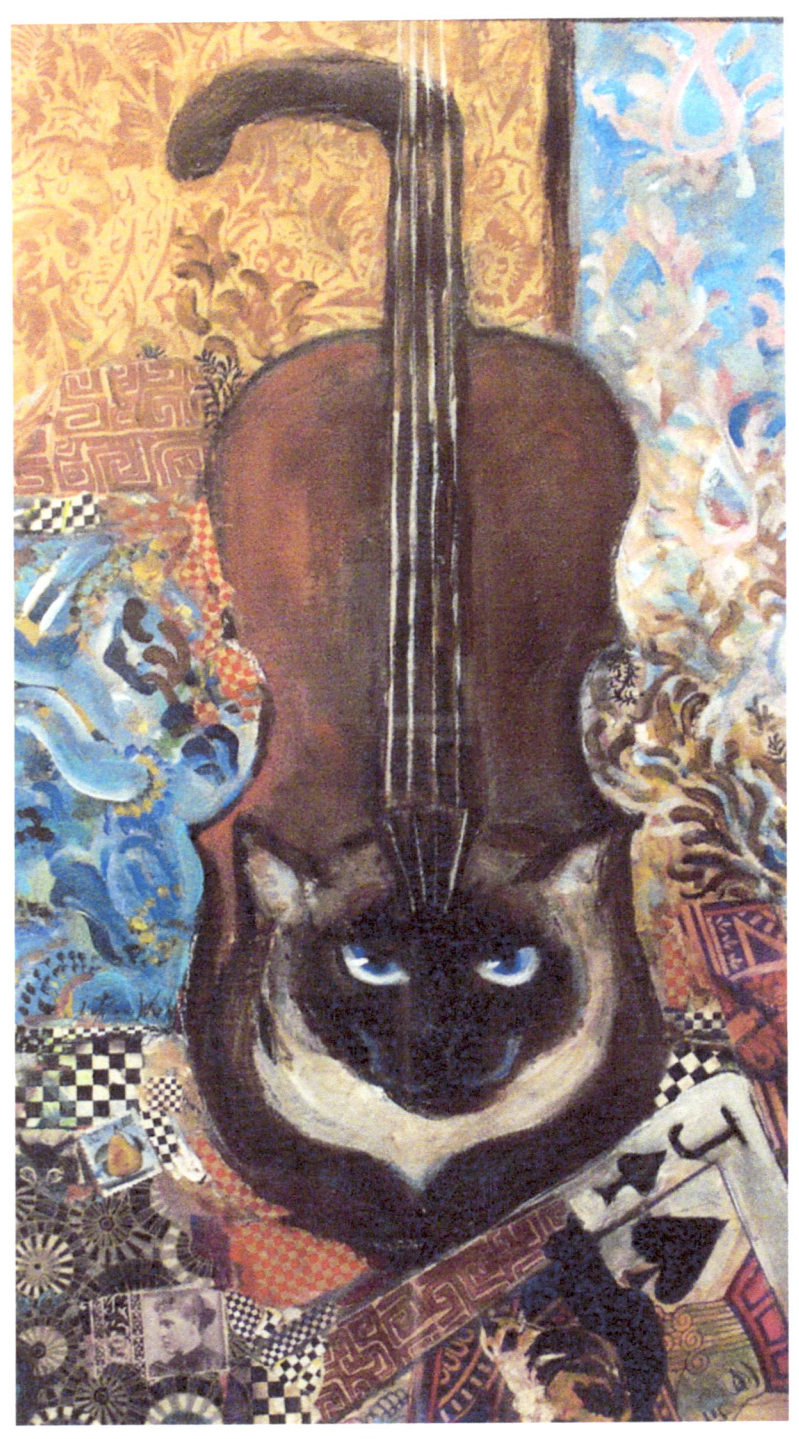

Violin Cat #4
22"x10"

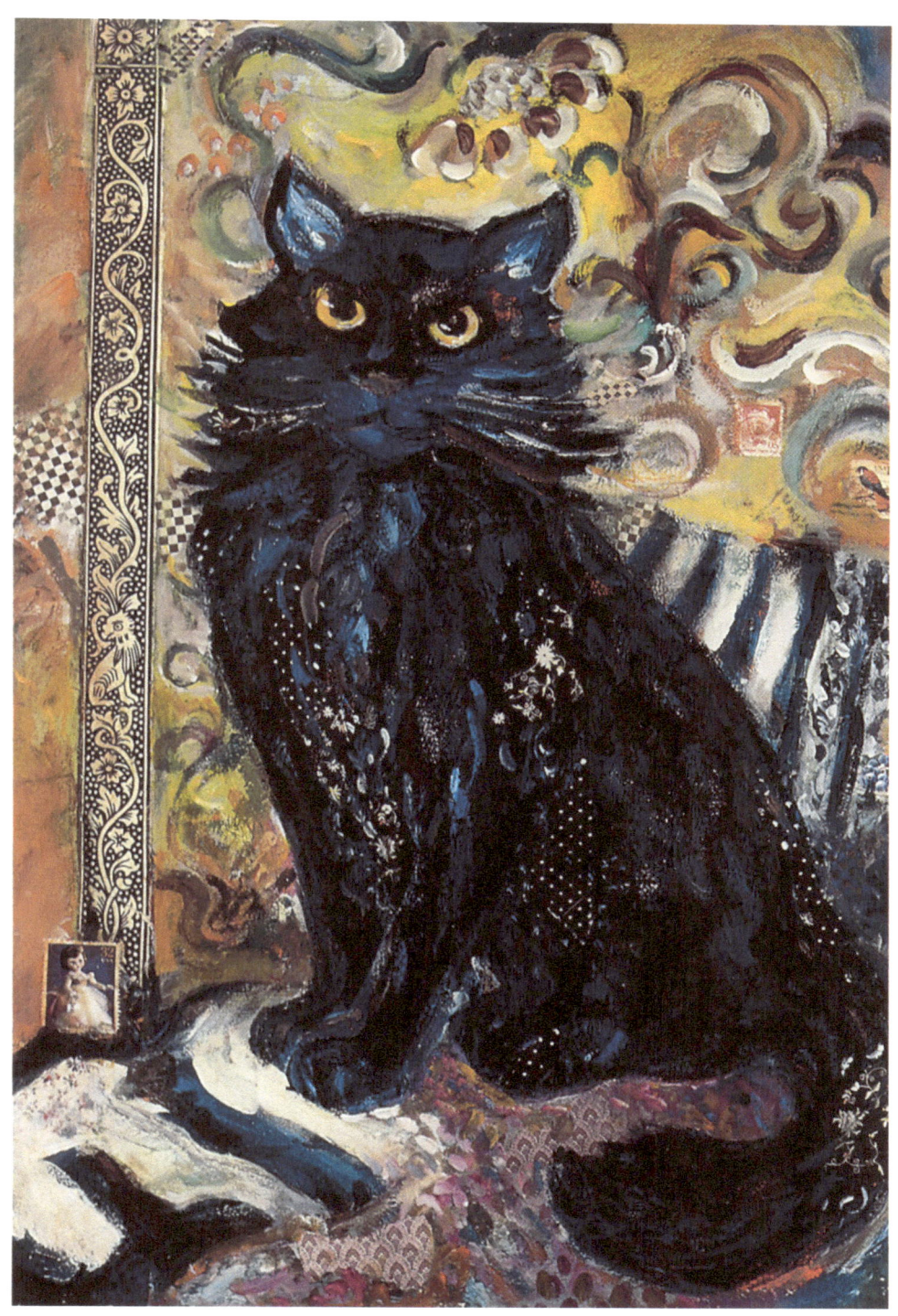

Tiffany Cat
22"x15"

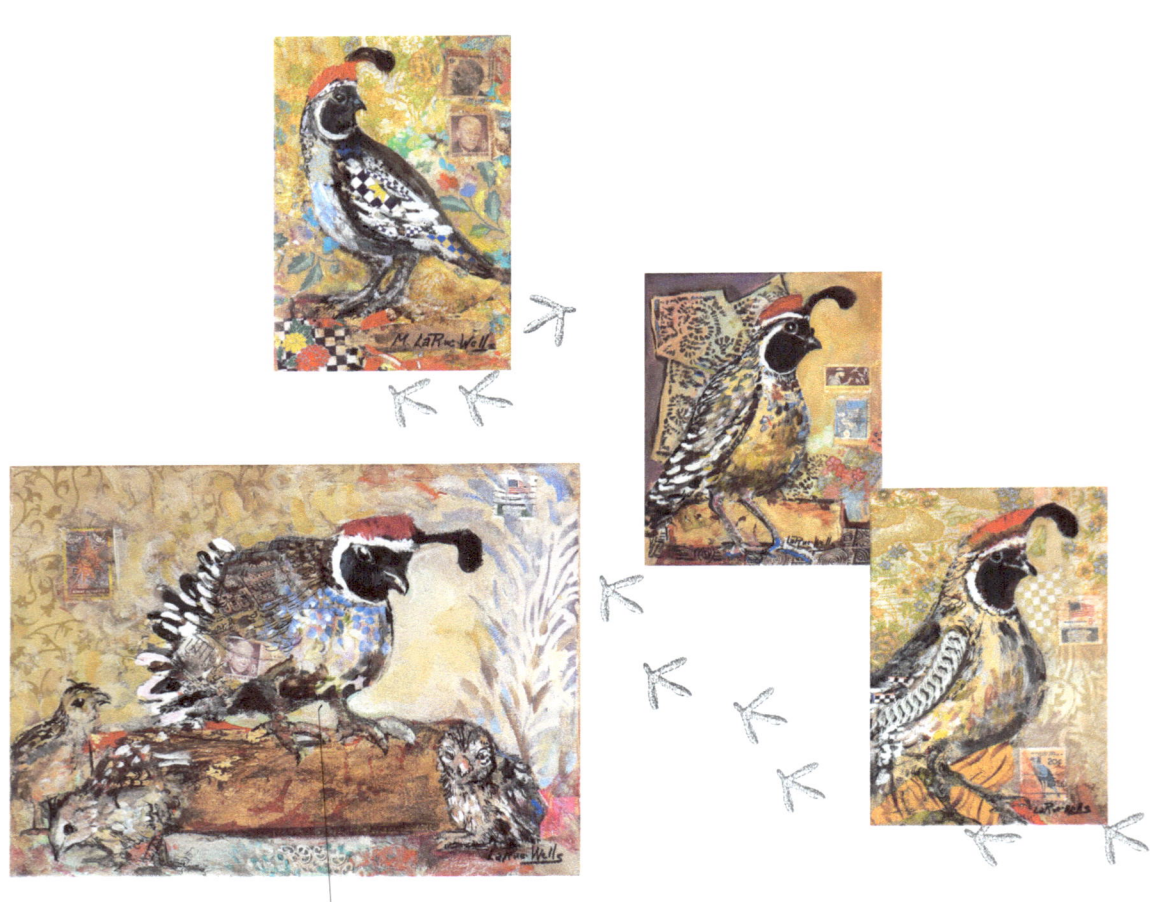

See more of Mary's creatures, critters and dramas at
www.marylaruewells.com

www.ingramcontent.com/pod-product-compliance
Lightning Source LLC
Chambersburg PA
CBHW050804180526
45159CB00004B/1542